Careers in Focus

AVIATION

Ferguson
An imprint of ☑® Facts On File

Careers in Focus: Aviation

Copyright © 2005 by Facts On File, Inc.

Ferguson
An imprint of Facts On File, Inc.
132 West 31st Street
New York NY 10001

Library of Congress Cataloging-in-Publication Data
Careers in focus. Aviation
   p. cm.
   Includes index
   ISBN 0-8160-5842-3 (hc : alk. paper)
   1. Aeronautics—Vocational guidance. I. Title: Aviation.
  TL561.C376 2005
  629.13'0023—dc22   2004013817

Ferguson books are available at special discounts when purchased in bulk quantities for businesses, associations, institutions, or sales promotions. Please call our Special Sales Department in New York at (212) 967-8800 or (800) 322-8755.

You can find Ferguson on the World Wide Web at http://www.fergpubco.com

Text design by David Strelecky

Printed in the United States of America

MP JT 10 9 8 7 6 5 4 3 2

This book is printed on acid-free paper.

Table of Contents

Introduction

Careers in Focus: Aviation describes a variety of careers in the aviation industry, at airports, flight schools, factories, customer service centers, travel agencies, shipping companies, and in military settings. These careers are as diverse in nature as they are in their earnings and educational requirements. Earnings range from minimum wage for entry-level airport service workers to $150,000 or more for pilots and some airport security workers. A few of these careers—such as airport food service worker and skycap—require little formal education, but are excellent starting points for a career in the industry. Other jobs, many of which are technical in nature, require some postsecondary training or an associate's degree. Examples of these careers include aeronautical and aerospace technicians, aircraft mechanics, and avionics technicians. The most advanced positions require either a minimum of a bachelor's degree (aerospace engineers, air traffic controllers, and avionics engineers) or a combination of postsecondary training and flight certification (flight instructors and pilots) from the Federal Aviation Administration.

The U.S. Department of Labor's *Career Guide to Industries* predicts that employment in the aerospace products and parts manufacturing industry will decrease by 18 percent through 2012. The air transportation industry is projected to grow by 12 percent through 2012—or 4 percent less than the average for all industries. The events of September 11, 2001, had a major impact on both the aerospace products and parts manufacturing industry and the air transportation industry. Layoffs, mergers, and bankruptcies hit both industries hard as the number of air passengers decreased.

The U.S. Department of Labor predicts that the employment decline in the manufacturing segment of the aviation industry will be partially offset by a growing demand for military aircraft and military aerospace equipment, which will be used in defensive and offensive operations in the United States and abroad.

The U.S. Department of Labor also predicts that, barring any future terrorist attacks on our aviation system, the airline industry will continue to suffer over the short term and then begin a slow recovery as passengers take to the skies again. Our growing population, an improving economy, and increases in international business and shipping should help the airline industry bounce back to pre-9/11 levels and provide good opportunities for workers in this field.

1

The articles in *Careers in Focus: Aviation* appear in Ferguson's *Encyclopedia of Careers and Vocational Guidance,* but have been updated and revised with the latest information from the U.S. Department of Labor, professional organizations, and other sources. In addition, articles about the following careers have been written specifically for this book: airport security personnel, airport service workers, aviation safety inspectors, flight instructors, ground services workers, and military pilots.

The **Quick Facts** section provides a brief summary of the career including recommended school subjects, personal skills, work environment, minimum educational requirements, salary ranges, certification or licensing requirements, and employment outlook. This section also provides acronyms and identification numbers for the following government classification indexes: the *Dictionary of Occupational Titles* (DOT), the *Guide for Occupational Exploration* (GOE), the National Occupational Classification (NOC) Index, and the Occupational Information Network (O*NET)-Standard Occupational Classification System (SOC) index. The DOT, GOE, and O*NET-SOC indexes have been created by the U.S. government; the NOC index is Canada's career-classification system. Readers can use the identification numbers listed in the Quick Facts section to access further information about a career. Print editions of the DOT (*Dictionary of Occupational Titles.* Indianapolis, Ind.: JIST Works, 1991) and GOE (*The Complete Guide for Occupational Exploration.* Indianapolis, Ind.: JIST Works, 1993) are available at libraries. Electronic versions of the NOC (http://www23.hrdc-drhc.gc.ca) and O*NET-SOC (http://online.onetcenter.org) are available on the World Wide Web. When no DOT, GOE, NOC, or O*NET-SOC numbers are present, this means that the U.S. Department of Labor or Human Resources Development Canada have not created a numerical designation for this career. In this instance, you will see the acronym "N/A," or not available.

The **Overview** section is a brief introductory description of the duties and responsibilities involved in this career. Oftentimes, a career may have a variety of job titles. When this is the case, alternative career titles are presented.

The **History** section describes the history of the particular job as it relates to the overall development of its industry or field.

The **Job** describes the primary and secondary duties of the job.

Requirements discusses high school and postsecondary education and training requirements, any certification or licensing that is necessary, and other personal requirements for success in the job.

Exploring offers suggestions on how to gain experience in or knowledge of the particular job before making a firm educational and financial commitment. The focus is on what can be done while still in high school (or in the early years of college) to gain a better understanding of the job.

The **Employers** section gives an overview of typical places of employment for the job.

Starting Out discusses the best ways to land that first job, be it through the college placement office, newspaper ads, or personal contacts.

The **Advancement** section describes what kind of career path to expect from the job and how to get there.

Earnings lists salary ranges and describes the typical fringe benefits.

The **Work Environment** section describes the typical surroundings and conditions of employment—whether indoors or outdoors, noisy or quiet, social or independent. This section also discusses typical hours worked, any seasonal fluctuations, and the stresses and strains of the job.

The **Outlook** section summarizes the job in terms of the general economy and industry projections. For the most part, Outlook information is obtained from the U.S. Bureau of Labor Statistics and is supplemented by information taken from professional associations. Job growth terms follow those used in the *Occupational Outlook Handbook*. Growth described as "much faster than the average" means an increase of 36 percent or more. Growth described as "faster than the average" means an increase of 21 to 35 percent. Growth described as "about as fast as the average" means an increase of 10 to 20 percent. Growth described as "more slowly than the average" means an increase of 3 to 9 percent. Growth described as "little or no change" means an increase of 0 to 2 percent. "Decline" means a decrease of 1 percent or more. Each article ends with **For More Information,** which lists organizations that provide career information on training, education, internships, scholarships, and job placement.

Careers in Focus: Aviation also includes photos, informative sidebars, and interviews with professionals in the field.

If you enjoy travelling by airplane, going to airports, meeting people from all over the world, or have an knack for mechanics or mathematics, there may be an exciting career in aviation waiting for you. Read about the careers in this varied field, and be sure to contact the organizations listed at the end of each article for more information.

Aeronautical and Aerospace Technicians

QUICK FACTS

School Subjects
Mathematics
Physics
Technical/shop

Personal Skills
Mechanical/manipulative
Technical/scientific

Work Environment
Primarily indoors
Primarily one location

Minimum Education Level
Associate's degree

Salary Range
$29,141 to $51,650 to
$73,480+

Certification or Licensing
Recommended

Outlook
More slowly than the average

DOT
002

GOE
05.01.04

NOC
N/A

O*NET-SOC
17-3021.00

OVERVIEW

Aeronautical and aerospace technicians design, construct, test, operate, and maintain the basic structures of aircraft, spacecraft, and propulsion and control systems. They work with scientists and engineers. Many aeronautical and aerospace technicians assist engineers in preparing equipment drawings, diagrams, blueprints, and scale models. They collect information, make computations, and perform laboratory tests. Their work may include working on various projects involving aerodynamics, structural design, flight-test evaluation, or propulsion problems. Other technicians estimate the cost of materials and labor required to manufacture the product, serve as manufacturers' field service technicians, and write technical materials. There are approximately 15,000 aeronautical and aerospace technicians employed in the United States.

HISTORY

Both aeronautical engineering and the aerospace industry were born in the early 20th century. The very earliest machine-powered and heavier-than-air aircraft, such as the first one flown by Wilbur and Orville Wright in 1903, were crudely constructed and often the result of costly and dangerous trial-and-error experimentation.

As government and industry took an interest in the possible applications of these inventions, however, knowledge of aircraft and the entire industry became more sophisticated. By 1908, for instance, the Wright brothers had received their first government military contract, and by 1909 the industry had expanded to include additional airplane producers, such as Glenn Curtiss in the United States and several others in France.

Aeronautical engineering and the aerospace industry have been radically transformed since those early days, mostly because of the demands of two world wars and the tremendous increases in scientific knowledge that have taken place since that time. Aviation and aerospace developments continued after the end of World War II. The factories and workers that built planes to support the war were in place and the industry took off, with the jet engine, rocket propulsion, supersonic flight, and manned voyages outside the earth's atmosphere among the major developments. As the industry evolved, aeronautical and aerospace engineers found themselves taking on increasingly larger projects and were more in need of trained and knowledgeable assistants to help them. Throughout the years, these assistants have been known as engineering aides, as engineering associates, and, most recently, as aerospace technicians and technologists. Their main task today is to take on assignments that require technical skills but do not necessarily require the scientist's or engineer's special training and education.

THE JOB

There are no clear-cut definitions of *aeronautical technology* and *aerospace technology;* in fact, many employers use the terms interchangeably. This lack of a clear distinction also occurs in education, where many schools and institutes offer similar courses under a variety of titles, such as aeronautical, aviation, or aerospace technology. In general, however, the term *aerospace industry* refers to manufacturers of all kinds of flying vehicles: from piston and jet-powered aircraft that fly inside the earth's atmosphere, to rockets, missiles, satellites, probes, and all kinds of manned and unmanned spacecraft that operate outside the earth's atmosphere. The term *aeronautics* is often used within the aerospace industry to refer specifically to mechanical flight inside the earth's atmosphere, especially to the design and manufacture of commercial passenger and freight aircraft, private planes, and helicopters.

The difference between technicians and technologists generally refers to their level of education. Technicians generally hold associate's degrees, while technologists hold bachelor's degrees in aeronautical technology.

Whether they work for a private company or for the federal government, aerospace technicians work side by side with engineers and scientists in all major phases of the design, production, and operation of aircraft and spacecraft technology. The aerospace technician position involves collecting and recording data, operating test equipment such as wind tunnels and flight simulators, devising tests to ensure quality control, modifying mathematical procedures to fit specific problems, laying out experimental circuits to test scientific theories, and evaluating experimental data for practical applications.

Aerospace physiological technicians operate devices used to train pilots and astronauts. These devices include pressure suits, pressure chambers, and ejection seats that simulate flying conditions. These technicians also operate other kinds of flight training equipment such as tow reels, radio equipment, and meteorological devices. They interview trainees about their medical histories, which helps detect evidence of conditions that would disqualify pilots or astronauts from further training.

Aircraft launch and recovery technicians work on aircraft carriers to operate, adjust, and repair launching and recovery equipment such as catapults, barricades, and arresting nets. They disassemble the launch and recovery equipment, replace defective parts, and keep track of all maintenance activities.

Avionics technicians repair, test, install, and maintain radar and radio equipment aboard aircraft and spacecraft.

Computer technicians assist mathematicians and subject specialists in checking and refining computations and systems, such as those required for predicting and determining orbits of spacecraft.

Drafting and design technicians convert the aeronautical engineer's specifications and rough sketches of aeronautical and aerospace equipment, such as electrical and mechanical devices, into accurate drawings. Skilled craft workers use these drawings to make parts for aircraft and spacecraft.

Electronics technicians assist engineers in the design, development, and modification of electronic and electromechanical systems. They assist in the calibration and operation of radar and photographic equipment and also operate, install, troubleshoot, and repair electronic testing equipment.

Engineering technicians assist with review and analysis of post-flight data, structural failure, and other factors that cause failure in flight vehicles.

Industrial engineering technicians assist engineers in preparing layouts of machinery and equipment, workflow plans, time-and-motion studies, and statistical studies and analyses of production costs to produce the most efficient use of personnel, materials, and machines.

Instrumentation technicians test, install, and maintain electronic, hydraulic, pneumatic, and optical instruments. These are used in aircraft systems and components in manufacturing as well as research and development. One important responsibility is to maintain their assigned research instruments. As a part of this maintenance, they test the instruments, take readings and calibration curves, and calculate correction factors for the instruments.

Liaison technicians check on the production of aircraft and spacecraft as they are being built for conformance to specifications, keep engineers informed as the manufacturing progresses, and investigate any engineering production problems that arise.

Mathematical technicians assist mathematicians, engineers, and scientists by performing computations involving the use of advanced mathematics.

Mechanical technicians use metalworking machines to assist in the manufacture of one-of-a-kind parts. They also assist in rocket-fin alignment, payload mating, weight and center-of-gravity measurements, and launch-tower erection.

Target aircraft technicians repair and maintain pilotless target aircraft. They assemble, repair, or replace aircraft parts such as cowlings, wings, and propeller assemblies and test aircraft engine operation.

REQUIREMENTS

High School

A strong science and mathematics background is essential for entry into this field. High school courses that will be useful in preparing a student for college-level study include algebra, trigonometry, physics, and chemistry. In addition to math and science, courses in social studies, economics, history, blueprint reading, drafting, and industrial and machine shop practice will provide a valuable background for a career in aerospace technology. Computer experience is also important. English, speech, and courses in the preparation of test reports and technical writing are extremely helpful to develop communication ability.

Postsecondary Training

There are a variety of training possibilities for potential aerospace technicians: two-, three-, or four-year programs at colleges or universities, junior or community colleges, technical institutes, vocational-technical schools, industry on-the-job training, or work-study programs in the military. Graduates from a two- or three-year program usually earn an associate's degree in engineering or science. Graduates from a four-year program earn a bachelor's degree in engineering or science; in addition, several colleges offer four-year degree programs in aeronautical technology. There are also many technical training schools, particularly in areas where the aerospace industry is most active, that offer training in aeronautical technology. However, many employers require graduates of such programs to complete a period of on-the-job training before they are granted full technician status. When selecting a school to attend, check the listings of such agencies as the Accreditation Board for Engineering and Technology and the regional accrediting associations for engineering colleges. Most employers prefer graduates from accredited schools.

In general, post–high school programs strengthen the student's background in science and mathematics, including pretechnical training. Beyond that, an interdisciplinary curriculum is more helpful than one that specializes in a narrow field. Other courses, which are basic to the work of the aeronautical scientist and engineer, should be part of a balanced program. These include basic physics, nuclear theory, chemistry, mechanics, and computers, including data-processing equipment and procedures.

Certification or Licensing
Only a few aerospace technician positions require licensing or certification; however, certificates issued by professional organizations do enhance the status of qualified engineering technicians. Certification is usually required of those working with nuclear-powered engines or testing radioactive sources, for those working on aircraft in some test programs, and in some safety-related positions. Technicians and technologists working in areas related to national defense, and especially those employed by government agencies, are usually required to carry security clearances.

Other Requirements
Aeronautical and aerospace technicians must be able to learn basic engineering skills. They should enjoy and be proficient in mathematics and the physical sciences and be able to visualize size, form, and function. The Aerospace Industries Association of America (AIA) advises that today's aerospace production worker must be strong in the basics of manufacturing, have a knowledge of statistics, and have the ability to work with computers.

EXPLORING

Visiting an aerospace research or manufacturing facility is one of the best ways to learn more about this field. Because there are many such facil-

Did You Know?

- In 2003, the U.S. aeronautical and aerospace industries had $147 billion in sales—a decrease of 4 percent from 2002.

- Approximately 618,000 people were employed in the aeronautical and aerospace industries in 2002; women held 109,000 of these jobs.

- The states of Washington and California offer the most aeronautical and aerospace jobs. Other states that offer strong employment opportunities include Kansas, Texas, Connecticut, and Arizona.

- In 2001, employees in this industry worked an average of 42.7 hours a week.

- Twenty-two percent of workers in these industries are union members—a percentage that is 7 percent higher than the national average for all occupations.

Sources: U.S. Department of Labor, Aerospace Industries Association

ities connected with the aerospace industry throughout the United States, there is sure to be one in nearly every area. The reference department of a local library can help you locate the nearest facility.

Finding part-time or summer employment at such a facility is, of course, one of the best ways to gain experience or learn more about the field. Such jobs aren't available for all students interested in the field, but you can still find part-time work that will give you practical experience, such as in a local machine shop or factory.

Students should not overlook the educational benefits of visiting local museums of science and technology or aircraft museums or displays. The National Air and Space Museum of the Smithsonian Institution in Washington, D.C., is one of the most comprehensive museums dedicated to aerospace. Some Air Force bases or naval air stations also offer tours to groups of interested students. Your teacher or career guidance counselor can arrange the tours.

The Junior Engineering Technical Society (JETS) provides students a chance to explore career opportunities in engineering and technology, enter academic competitions, and design model structures. JETS administers a competition that allows students to use their technology skills. The Tests of Engineering, Aptitude, Mathematics, and Science is an open-book, open-discussion engineering problem competition. If your school doesn't have a JETS chapter, check with other schools in your area; sometimes smaller schools can form cooperatives to offer such programs.

EMPLOYERS

Aeronautical and aerospace technicians and technologists are principally employed by government agencies, commercial airlines, educational institutions, and aerospace manufacturing companies. Most technicians employed by manufacturing companies engage in research, development, and design; the remainder work in production, sales, engineering, installation and maintenance, and other related fields. Those employed by government and educational institutions are normally assigned to do research and specific problem-solving tasks. Airlines employ technicians to supervise maintenance operations and the development of procedures for new equipment.

STARTING OUT

The best way for students to obtain an aeronautical or aerospace technician's job is through their college or university's job placement office. Many manufacturers maintain recruiting relationships with schools in their area. Jobs may also be obtained through state employment offices, newspaper advertisements, applications for government employment, and industry work-study programs offered by many aircraft companies.

ADVANCEMENT

Aeronautical and aerospace technicians continue to learn on the job. As they gain experience in specialized areas, employers turn to them to solve problems, create new techniques, devise new designs, or develop practice from theory.

Most advancement involves taking on additional responsibilities. For example, with experience, a technician may take on supervisory responsibilities overseeing several trainees, assistant technicians, or others. Such a technician may also be assigned independent responsibilities, including some tasks usually assigned to an engineer. Technicians who have outgoing personalities and a good working knowledge of their company's equipment may become company sales or technical representatives. Technicians seeking further advancement are advised to continue their education. With additional formal education, a technician may become an aeronautical or aerospace engineer.

EARNINGS

Aerospace technology is a broad field, so earnings vary depending on a technician's specialty, educational preparation, and work experience. According to the U.S. Department of Labor, the average annual salary for aerospace technicians was $51,650 in 2002. Salaries ranged from less than $34,820 to more than $73,480. Beyond that, salaries varied depending on specialty. For example, aerospace engineering and operations technicians employed in the aerospace products and parts manufacturing industry earned median salaries of $54,530 in 2002. For aircraft mechanics, the average salary was $43,077. Avionics technicians earned salaries that ranged from less than $29,141 to $56,160 or more.

Benefits depend on employers but usually include paid vacations and holidays, sick pay, health insurance, and a retirement plan. Salary increases will likely be held to a minimum over the next few years as the industry struggles to achieve a new balance after years of cutbacks. Nearly all companies offer some form of tuition reimbursement for further education. Some offer cooperative programs with local schools, combining classroom training with practical paid experience.

WORK ENVIRONMENT

The aerospace industry, with its strong emphasis on quality and safety, is a very safe place to work. Special procedures and equipment make otherwise hazardous jobs extremely safe. The range of work covered means that the technicians can work in small teams in specialized research laboratories or in test areas that are large and sterile.

Aerospace technicians are at the launch pad, involved in fueling and checkout procedures, and back in the blockhouse sitting at an electronic console. They work in large test facilities or in specialized shops, designing and fabricating equipment. They travel to test sites or tracking stations to construct facilities or troubleshoot systems. Working conditions vary with the assignment, but the work climate is always challenging, and coworkers are well-trained, competent people.

Aeronautical technicians may perform inside activities involving confined detail work, they may work outside, or they may combine both situations. Aeronautical and aerospace technicians work in many situations: alone, in small teams, or in large groups. Commonly, technicians participate in team projects, which are coordinated efforts of scientists, engineers, and technicians working on specific assignments. They concentrate on the practical aspects of the project and must get along well with and interact cooperatively with the scientists responsible for the theoretical aspects of the project.

Aerospace technicians must be able to perform under deadline pressure, meet strict requirements and rigid specifications, and deal with potentially hazardous situations. They must be willing and flexible enough to acquire new knowledge and techniques to adjust to the rapidly changing technology. In addition, technicians need persistence and tenacity, especially when engaged in experimental and research tasks. They must be responsible, reliable, and willing to accept greater responsibility.

Aerospace technology is never far from the public's attention, and aeronautical technicians have the additional satisfaction of knowing that they are viewed as being engaged in vital and fascinating work.

OUTLOOK

The *Career Guide to Industries* predicts that the aerospace products and parts manufacturing segment of the civilian aerospace industry is expected to decline by 18 percent through 2012 as a result of a severe reduction in orders for commercial transport aircraft. Employment in the military aircraft sector is expected to be better during this same time period as a result of our nation's need for more military aircraft, aerospace equipment, and related materials.

Many manufacturers in the aerospace industry have responded to the decline that occurred during the 1990s by broadening their production to include other areas of technology. The AIA predicts aerospace companies will be looking for qualified technicians in fields such as laser optics, mission operations, hazardous materials procedures, production planning, materials testing, computer-aided design, and robotic operations and programming.

FOR MORE INFORMATION

For a listing of accredited technology programs, check the website or contact

Accreditation Board for Engineering and Technology
111 Market Place, Suite 1050
Baltimore, MD 21202-4012
Tel: 410-347-7700
http://www.abet.org

For information on financial aid, contact
Aerospace Education Foundation
1501 Lee Highway
Arlington, VA 22209-1198
Tel: 703-247-5839
Email: aefstaff@aef.org
http://www.aef.org

Contact AIA for publications with information on aerospace technologies, careers, and space.
**Aerospace Industries Association
   of America**
1000 Wilson Boulevard, Suite 1700
Arlington, VA 22209-3901
Tel: 703-358-1000
http://www.aia-aerospace.org

For career information and details on student branches of this organization, contact
**American Institute of Aeronautics and
   Astronautics**
1801 Alexander Bell Drive, Suite 500
Reston, VA 20191-4344
Tel: 800-639-2422
http://www.aiaa.org

For information on educational programs and to purchase a copy of
Engineering: Go For It, *contact*
**American Society for Engineering
   Education**
1818 N Street, NW
Washington, DC 20036
Tel: 202-331-3500
http://www.asee.org

For career and scholarship information, contact
**General Aviation Manufacturers
   Association**
1400 K Street, NW, Suite 801
Washington, DC 20005
Tel: 202-393-1500
http://www.generalaviation.org

JETS has career information and offers high school students the opportunity to "try on" engineering through a number of programs and competitions. For more information, contact

Junior Engineering Technical Society
1420 King Street, Suite 405
Alexandria, VA 22314-2794
Tel: 703-548-5387
Email: info@jets.org
http://www.jets.org

SEDS is an international organization of high school and college students dedicated to promoting interest in space. The United States national headquarters are located at the Massachusetts Institute of Technology.

Students for the Exploration and Development of Space (SEDS)
MIT Room W20-445
77 Massachusetts Avenue
Cambridge, MA 02139-4307
Email: mitseds-officers@mit
http://www.mit.edu/~mitseds

For more information on career choices and schools, contact

Aerospace Industries Association of Canada
60 Queen Street, Suite 1200
Ottawa, ON K1P 5Y7 Canada
Tel: 613-232-4297
Email: info@aiac.ca
http://www.aiac.ca

Aerospace Engineers

OVERVIEW

Aerospace engineering encompasses the fields of aeronautical (aircraft) and astronautical (spacecraft) engineering. *Aerospace engineers* work in teams to design, build, and test machines that fly within the earth's atmosphere and beyond. Although aerospace science is a very specialized discipline, it is also considered one of the most diverse. This field of engineering draws from such subjects as physics, mathematics, earth science, aerodynamics, and biology. Some aerospace engineers specialize in designing one complete machine, perhaps a commercial aircraft, whereas others focus on separate components such as for missile guidance systems. There are approximately 78,000 aerospace engineers working in the United States.

HISTORY

The roots of aerospace engineering can be traced as far back as when people first dreamed of being able to fly. Thousands of years ago, the Chinese developed kites and later experimented with gunpowder as a source of propulsion. In the 15th century, Renaissance artist Leonardo da Vinci created drawings of two devices that were designed to fly. One, the ornithopter, was supposed to fly the way birds do, by flapping its wings; the other was designed as a rotating screw, closer in form to today's helicopter.

In 1783, Joseph and Jacques Montgolfier of France designed the first hot-air balloon that could be used for manned flight. In 1799, an English baron, Sir George Cayley, designed an aircraft that was one of the first not to be considered "lighter than air," as balloons were. He developed a fixed-wing structure that led to his creation of

QUICK FACTS

School Subjects
Mathematics
Physics

Personal Skills
Mechanical/manipulative
Technical/scientific

Work Environment
Primarily indoors
Primarily one location

Minimum Education Level
Bachelor's degree

Salary Range
$48,028 to $72,750 to
$105,060+

Certification or Licensing
Required

Outlook
Decline

DOT
002

GOE
05.01.07

NOC
2146

O*NET-SOC
17-2011.00

the first glider in 1849. Much experimentation was performed in gliders and the science of aerodynamics through the late 1800s. In 1903, the first mechanically powered and controlled flight was completed in a craft designed by Orville and Wilbur Wright. The big boost in airplane development occurred during World War I. In the early years of the war, aeronautical engineering encompassed a variety of engineering skills applied toward the development of flying machines. Civil engineering principles were used in structural design, while early airplane engines were devised by automobile engineers. Aerodynamic design itself was primarily empirical, with many answers coming from liquid flow concepts established in marine engineering.

The evolution of the airplane continued during both world wars, with steady technological developments in materials science, propulsion, avionics, and stability and control. Airplanes became larger and faster. Airplanes are commonplace today, but commercial flight became a frequent mode of transportation only as recently as the 1960s and 1970s.

Robert Goddard developed and flew the first liquid-propelled rocket in 1926. The technology behind liquid propulsion continued to evolve, and the first U.S. liquid rocket engine was tested in 1938. More sophisticated rockets were eventually created to enable aircraft to be launched into space. The world's first artificial satellite, *Sputnik I*, was launched by the Soviets in 1957. In 1961, President John F. Kennedy urged the United States to be the first country to put a man on the moon; on July 20, 1969, astronauts Neil Armstrong and Edwin Aldrin Jr. accomplished that goal.

Today, aerospace engineers design spacecraft such as space shuttles and rockets, which explore beyond the earth's atmosphere. Engineers create missiles and military aircraft of many types, such as fighters, bombers, observers, and transports. Today's engineers go beyond the dreams of merely learning to fly. For example, in 1998 the United States and 15 other countries began a series of joint missions into space to assemble a planned International Space Station. On the ground, space professionals, including aerospace engineers, are playing a vital role in developing equipment that will be used on the station.

THE JOB

Although the creation of aircraft and spacecraft involve professionals from many branches of engineering (for example, materials, electrical, and mechanical), aerospace engineers in particular are responsible for the total design of the craft, including its shape, performance, propulsion, and guidance-control system. In the field of aerospace engineering, professional responsibilities vary widely depending on the specific job description. *Aeronautical engineers* work specifically with aircraft systems, and *astronautical engineers* specialize in spacecraft systems.

Throughout their education and training, aerospace engineers thoroughly learn the complexities involved in how materials and structures perform under tremendous stress. In general, they are called upon to apply their knowledge of the following subjects: propulsion, aerodynamics, thermodynamics, fluid mechanics, flight mechanics, and structural analysis. Less technically scientific issues must also be dealt with, such as cost analysis, reliability studies, maintainability, operations research, marketing, and management.

There are many professional titles given to certain aerospace engineers. *Analytical engineers* use engineering and mathematical theory to solve questions that arise during the design phase. *Stress analysts* determine how the weight and loads of structures behave under a variety of conditions. This analysis is performed with computers and complex formulas.

Computational fluid dynamic (CFD) engineers use sophisticated high-speed computers to develop models used in the study of fluid dynamics. Using simulated systems, they determine how elements flow around objects; simulation saves time and money and eliminates risks involved with actual testing. As computers become more complex, so do the tasks of the CFD engineer.

Design aerospace engineers draw from the expertise of many other specialists. They devise the overall structure of components and entire crafts, meeting the specifications developed by those more specialized in aerodynamics, astrodynamics, and structural engineering. Design engineers use computer-aided design programs for many of their tasks. *Manufacturing aerospace engineers* develop the plans for producing the complex components that make up aircraft and spacecraft. They work with the designers to ensure that the plans are economically feasible and will produce efficient, effective components.

Materials aerospace engineers determine the suitability of the various materials that are used to produce aerospace vehicles. Aircraft and spacecraft require the appropriate tensile strength, density, and rigidity for the particular environments they are subjected to. Determining how materials such as steel, glass, and even chemical compounds react to temperature and stress is an important part of the materials engineer's responsibilities.

Quality control is a task that aerospace engineers perform throughout the development, design, and manufacturing processes. The finished product must be evaluated for its reliability, vulnerability, and how it is to be maintained and supported.

Marketing and sales aerospace engineers work with customers, usually industrial corporations and the government, informing them of product performance. They act as a liaison between the technical engineers and the clients to help ensure that the products delivered are performing as planned. Sales engineers also need to anticipate the needs of the customer, as far ahead as possible, to inform their companies of potential marketing opportunities. They also keep abreast of their competitors and need to understand how to structure contracts effectively.

REQUIREMENTS

High School

While in high school, follow a college preparatory program. Doing well in mathematics and science classes is vital if you want to pursue a career in any type of engineering field. The American Society for Engineering Education advises students to take calculus and trigonometry in high school, as well as laboratory science classes. Such courses will help you develop problem-solving skills, which are essential in any type of engineering.

Postsecondary Training

Aerospace engineers need a bachelor's degree to enter the field. More advanced degrees are necessary for those interested in teaching or research and development positions.

While a major in aerospace engineering is the norm, other majors are acceptable. For example, the National Aeronautics and Space Administration recommends a degree in any of a variety of disciplines, including biomedical engineering, ceramics engineering, chemistry, industrial engineering, materials science, metallurgy, optical engineering, and oceanography. You should make sure the college you choose has an accredited engineering program. The Accreditation Board for Engineering and Technology (ABET) sets minimum education standards for programs in these fields. Graduation from an ABET-accredited school is a requirement for becoming licensed in many states, so it is important to select an accredited school. Currently, approximately 250 colleges and universities offer ABET-accredited engineering programs. Visit ABET's website (http://www.abet.org) for a listing of accredited schools.

Some aerospace engineers complete master's degrees and even doctoral work before entering this field. Advanced degrees can significantly increase an engineer's earnings. Students continuing on to graduate school will study research and development, with a thesis required for a master's degree and a dissertation for a doctorate. About one-third of all aerospace engineers go on to graduate school to get a master's degree.

Certification or Licensing

All states require engineers to be licensed. There are two levels of licensing for engineers. Professional engineers (PEs) have graduated from an accredited engineering curriculum, have four years of engineering experience, and have passed a written exam. Engineering graduates need not wait until they have four years experience, however, to start the licensure process. Those who pass the Fundamentals of Engineering examination after graduating are called engineers in training (EITs) or engineer interns or intern engineers. The EIT certification usually is valid for 10 years. After acquiring suitable work experience, EITs can take the second examination, the Principles and Practice of Engineering exam, to gain full PE licensure.

In order to ensure that aerospace engineers are kept up to date on their quickly changing field, many states have imposed continuing education requirements for relicensure.

Other Requirements

Aerospace engineers should enjoy completing detailed work, problem solving, and participating in group efforts. Mathematical, science, and computer skills are a must. Equally important, however, are the abilities to communicate ideas, share in teamwork, and visualize the forms and functions of structures. Curiosity, inventiveness, and the willingness to continue learning from experiences are excellent qualities to have for this type of work.

EXPLORING

If you like to work on model airplanes and rockets, you may be good candidate for an aerospace engineering career. Consider working on special research assignments supervised by your science and math teachers for helpful experience. You may also want to try working on cars and boats, which provides a good opportunity to discover more about aerodynamics. A part-time job with a local manufacturer can give you some exposure to product engineering and development.

Exciting opportunities are often available at summer camps and academic programs throughout the country. For instance, the University of North Dakota (see address listed at the end of this article) presents an aerospace camp focusing on study and career exploration that includes instruction in model rocketry and flight. However, admission to the camp is competitive; the camp usually consists of two eight-day programs for 32 students each.

It is also a good idea to join a science club while in high school. For example, the Junior Engineering Technical Society provides members with opportunities to enter academic competitions, explore career opportunities, and design model structures. Contact information is available at the end of this article.

*Aerospace America (*http://www.aiaa.org/aerospace), published by the American Institute of Aeronautics and Astronautics, is a helpful magazine for exploring careers in aerospace. You should also check out *Engineering: Your Future* (http://www.asee.org/precollege) at the American Society for Engineering Education's website. It offers general information about careers in engineering, as well as answers to frequently asked questions about engineering.

EMPLOYERS

The U.S. Department of Labor reports that approximately 78,000 aerospace engineers are employed in the United States. Many aircraft-related engineering jobs are found in Texas, Washington, Florida, and California, where large aerospace companies are located. Almost half of all aerospace engineers work in the aircraft and parts, guided missile, and space vehicle industries. Government agencies, such as the Department of Defense and the National Aeronautics and Space Administration, employ approximately 10 percent of aerospace engineers. Other employers include engineering services, research and testing services, and electronics manufacturers.

STARTING OUT

Many students begin their careers while completing their studies through work-study arrangements that sometimes turn into full-time jobs. Most aerospace manufacturers actively recruit engineering students, conducting on-campus interviews and other activities to locate the best candidates. Students preparing to graduate can also send out resumes to companies active in the aerospace industry and arrange interviews. Many colleges and universities also staff job placement centers, which are often good places to find leads for new job openings.

Students can also apply directly to agencies of the federal government concerned with aerospace development and implementation.

Applications can be made through the Office of Personnel Management or through an agency's own hiring department.

Professional associations, such as the National Society of Professional Engineers and the American Institute of Aeronautics and Astronautics, offer job placement services, including career advice, job listings, and training. Their Web addresses are listed at the end of this article.

ADVANCEMENT

As in most engineering fields, there tends to be a hierarchy of workers in the various divisions of aerospace engineering. This is true in research, design and development, production, and teaching. In an entry-level job, one is considered simply an engineer, perhaps a *junior engineer*. After a certain amount of experience is gained, depending on the position, one moves on to work as a *project engineer,* supervising others. Then, as a managing engineer, one has more responsibilities over a number of project engineers and their teams. At the top of the hierarchy is the position of *chief engineer,* which involves authority over managing engineers and additional decision-making responsibilities.

As engineers move up the career ladder, the type of responsibilities they have tend to change. Junior engineers are highly involved in technical matters and scientific problem solving. As managers and chiefs, engineers have the responsibilities of supervising, cost analyzing, and relating with clients.

All engineers must continue to learn and study technological progress throughout their careers. It is important to keep abreast of engineering advancements and trends by reading industry journals and taking courses. Such courses are offered by professional associations or colleges. In aerospace engineering especially, changes occur rapidly, and those who seek promotions must be prepared. Those who are employed by colleges and universities must continue teaching and conducting research if they want to have tenured (more guaranteed) faculty positions.

EARNINGS

In 2002, the average salary for all aerospace engineers was about $72,750 per year, according to the U.S. Department of Labor. The highest 10 percent earned more than $105,060 annually. Highly experienced engineers employed by the federal government earned an average salary of $81,830. Federal employees often enjoy greater job security and often more generous vacation and retirement benefits.

Top Employment Sectors and Earnings for Aerospace Engineers

Industry Sector	Employment	Annual Mean Earnings
Aerospace product and parts manufacturing	44,000	$71,840
Federal government	7,320	$81,580
Architectural and engineering services	5,150	$79,270
Electronic instrument manufacturing	4,340	$81,280
Technical and trade schools	1,780	$74,820

Source: U.S. Department of Labor

Aerospace engineers with bachelor's degrees earned average starting salaries of $48,028 per year, according to a 2003 salary survey conducted by the National Association of Colleges and Employers. With a master's degree, candidates were offered $61,162, and with a Ph.D., $68,406.

All engineers can expect to receive vacation and sick pay, paid holidays, health insurance, life insurance, and retirement programs.

WORK ENVIRONMENT

Aerospace engineers work in various settings depending on their job description. Those involved in research and design usually work in a traditional office setting. They spend considerable time at computers and drawing boards. Engineers involved with the testing of components and structures often work outside at test sites or in laboratories where controlled testing conditions can be created.

In the manufacturing area of the aerospace industry, engineers often work on the factory floor itself, assembling components and making sure that they conform to design specifications. This job requires much walking around large production facilities, such as aircraft factories or spacecraft assembly plants.

Engineers are sometimes required to travel to other locations to consult with companies that make materials and other needed components. Others travel to remote test sites to observe and participate in flight testing.

Aerospace engineers are also employed with the Federal Aviation Administration and commercial airline companies. These engineers perform a variety of duties, including performance analysis and crash investigations. Companies that are involved with satellite communications need the expertise of aerospace engineers to better interpret the many aspects of the space environment and the problems involved with getting a satellite launched into space.

OUTLOOK

Overall, employment in this field is expected to decline through 2012, according to the U.S. Department of Labor. The aerospace industry has gone through difficult times since the late 1980s, and more job losses are predicted for the immediate future. Reduced or stagnant space program budgets, the recession of the early 1990s, and the continuing wave of corporate downsizing have all combined to cut severely into the aerospace industry.

A slowdown in airline traffic and a decrease in orders for new commercial aircraft will limit job opportunities for aerospace engineers employed in the private sector. Job opportunities for aerospace engineers employed by the government will be better. In recent years, defense spending budgets have been increased to build up the armed forces. More aerospace engineers will be needed to repair and add to the current air fleet, as well as to improve defense technology. Engineers are also needed to help make commercial aircraft safer, designing and installing reinforced cockpit doors and onboard security screening equipment to protect pilots, crew, and commercial passengers.

Despite cutbacks in the space program, the development of new space technology and increasing commercial uses for that technology will continue to require qualified engineers. Facing reduced demand in the United States, aerospace companies are increasing their sales overseas, and depending on the world economy and foreign demand, this new market could create a demand for new workers in the industry.

Although the number of actual aerospace engineering jobs is expected to decline through 2012, opportunities for new aerospace engineers should be good as a result of declining enrollments in aerospace engineering programs and a large number of expected retirements during this time period. These openings are expected to account for most of the new jobs in the industry, but job satisfaction and longevity are high, so turnover is usually low.

FOR MORE INFORMATION

For a list of accredited schools and colleges, contact
Accreditation Board for Engineering and
    Technology
111 Market Place, Suite 1050
Baltimore, MD 21202-4102
Tel: 410-347-7700
http://www.abet.org

For information about scholarships, colleges, and career opportunities, contact
Aerospace Education Foundation
1501 Lee Highway
Arlington, VA 22209-1198
Tel: 703-247-5839
Email: aefstaff@aef.org
http://www.aef.org

Contact AIA for publications with information on aerospace technologies, careers, and space.
Aerospace Industries Association of America
1000 Wilson Boulevard, Suite 1700
Arlington, VA 22209-3901
Tel: 703-358-1000
http://www.aia-aerospace.org

For career information and details on student branches of this organization, contact
American Institute of Aeronautics and
    Astronautics
1801 Alexander Bell Drive, Suite 500
Reston, VA 20191-4344
Tel: 800-639-2422
http://www.aiaa.org

For information on educational programs and to purchase a copy of Engineering: Go For It, *contact*
American Society for Engineering Education
1818 N Street, NW
Washington, DC 20036
Tel: 202-331-3500
http://www.asee.org

For information on careers and student competitions, contact
Junior Engineering Technical Society
1420 King Street, Suite 405
Alexandria, VA 22314
Tel: 703-548-5387
Email: info@jets.org
http://www.jets.org

For career and licensing information, contact
National Society of Professional Engineers
1420 King Street
Alexandria, VA 22314-2794
Tel: 703-684-2800
http://www.nspe.org/students

For information on aerospace programs and summer camps, contact
University of North Dakota
John D. Odergard School of Aerospace Sciences
PO Box 9007
Grand Forks, ND 58202-9007
Tel: 800-258-1525
http://www.aero.und.edu

Agricultural Pilots

OVERVIEW

Agricultural pilots, also called *ag pilots* and *aerial applicators,* perform flying jobs related to the farming industry. They are skilled professionals who operate aircraft for such purposes as transporting cargo to market, aerial applications (also known as crop dusting), hauling feed, or planting seed. In addition to flying aircraft, agricultural pilots are responsible for performing a variety of safety-related tasks involving both the aircraft and the cargo. They may be self-employed or work for large pest control companies or government agencies. There are approximately 3,000 agricultural pilots employed in the United States.

HISTORY

The history of agricultural aviation is, naturally, tied to that of modern aviation. This period is generally considered to have begun with the flight of Orville and Wilbur Wright's heavier-than-air machine on December 17, 1903. On that day, the Wright brothers flew their machine four times and became the first airplane pilots. In the early days of aviation, the pilot's job was quite different from that of the pilot of today. As he flew the plane, for example, Orville Wright was lying on his stomach in the middle of the bottom wing of the plane. There was a strap across his hips, and to turn the plane, he had to tilt his hips from side to side—hardly the way today's pilot makes a turn.

The aviation industry developed rapidly as designers raced to improve upon the Wright brothers' design. During the early years of flight, many aviators earned a living as "barnstormers," entertaining people with stunts and taking passengers on short flights around the countryside. As airplanes became more dependable, they were adapted for a variety of purposes such as use in the military and for the United States government-run air mail service. According to the National Agricultural Aviation Association, the first time a plane was used to spread pesticide was in 1921. In an experiment conducted by the military, lead arsenate dust was spread by plane to stop a moth infestation in Ohio. By 1923 crop dusting was being done on a commercial basis.

Today planes used for agricultural aviation are specifically designed for that purpose. They can carry hundreds of gallons of pesticides and are equipped with the latest technology, such as Global Positioning System (GPS). Unlike the crop-dusting process of the past, which used dry chemicals, today's process typically involves liquid pesticides and other controlling products as well as nutrition sprays. Advances in agricultural aviation have allowed U.S. farms to become increasingly productive.

THE JOB

Agricultural pilots perform a number of duties that benefit the farming industry. They assist farmers in the prevention of crop damage. Some work for pest control companies while others are self-employed. In farm work, agricultural pilots spray chemicals over crops and orchards to fertilize them, control plant diseases or weeds, and control pests. They also drop seeds into fields to grow crops.

Before agricultural pilots begin the process of spraying farmland, they must survey the area for buildings, hills, power lines, and other obstacles and hazards. They must also notify residents and businesses in the general area that they will spray so that people and animals can be moved away from target areas.

Some agricultural pilots, particularly those who work for pest control companies, may mix their own chemicals, using their knowledge of what mixture may be best for certain types of plants, plant or soil conditions, or pest problems.

Agricultural pilots fly small, turboprop planes, which are slower compared to larger, transport craft, but which are good for flying close to the ground and for carrying heavy loads. They must fly close to the ground, often only a few feet above a crop, so that they will only hit designated areas with the chemicals.

Agricultural pilots help farmers by dropping food over pastures. They may photograph wildlife or count game animals for conservation programs. And their work also extends into forests, fields, and swamps, where herbicides and insecticides are needed. They also fight forest fires by dumping water or fire-retardant materials over burning areas.

No matter what the job, pilots must determine weather and flight conditions, make sure that sufficient fuel is on board to complete the flight safely, and verify the maintenance status of the airplane before each flight. They perform system checks to test the proper functioning of instrumentation and electronic and mechanical systems on the plane.

Once all of these preflight duties are done, the pilot taxis the aircraft to the designated runway and prepares for takeoff. Takeoff speeds must be calculated based on the aircraft's weight, which is affected by the weight of the cargo being carried.

During flights, agricultural pilots must constantly be aware of their surroundings since they fly so close to the ground and frequently are near hazards such as power lines. They need good judgment to deal with any emergency situations that might arise. They monitor aircraft systems, keep an eye on the weather conditions, and perform the job of the flight, such as spraying fertilizer.

Once the pilot has landed and taxied to the appropriate area, he or she follows a "shutdown" checklist of procedures. Pilots also keep logs of their flight hours. Those who are self-employed or work for smaller companies are typically responsible for refueling the airplane, performing maintenance, and keeping business records.

REQUIREMENTS

High School
There are a number of classes you can take in high school to help prepare you for becoming a pilot. You should take science classes, such as chemistry and physics, as well as mathematics, such as algebra and geometry. Take computer classes to familiarize yourself with various programs. Since you will be responsible for the maintenance and care of a plane, you may also benefit from taking an electronics shop class or other shop class where you get to work on engines. Take English classes to improve your research and writing skills. Throughout your career you will need to study flying or repair manuals, file reports, and communicate with customers. Since you may be responsible for record keeping, take business or accounting classes. If your school offers agriculture classes, take any that will teach you about soils, crops, and growing methods.

Postsecondary Training

Many companies that employ pilots prefer to hire candidates with at least two years of college training. Courses in engineering, meteorology, physics, mathematics, and agriculture are helpful in preparing for this career. In addition to these courses, you will need training as a pilot. There are approximately 600 civilian flying schools certified by the Federal Aviation Administration (FAA), including some colleges and universities that offer degree credit for pilot training. A number of schools offer training specifically in agricultural aviation. Some people take up this career after leaving the military, where they trained as pilots.

Certification or Licensing

Agricultural pilots must hold a commercial pilot's license from the FAA. A fairly long and rigorous process is involved in obtaining a commercial license. The first step in this process is to receive flying instruction.

If you are 16 or over and can pass the rigid mandatory physical examination, you may apply for permission to take flying instruction. This instruction consists of classroom education and flight training from a FAA-certified flight instructor.

Before you make your first solo flight, you must get a medical certificate (certifying that you are in good health) and an instructor-endorsed student pilot certificate. In order to get the student pilot certificate, you must pass a test given by the flight instructor. This test will have questions about FAA rules as well as questions about the model and make of the aircraft you will fly. If you pass the test and the instructor feels you are prepared to make a solo flight, the instructor will endorse your pilot certificate and logbook.

To apply for a private pilot's license, you must take a written examination. To qualify for it, you must be at least 17 years of age, successfully fulfill a solo flying requirement of 20 hours or more, and meet instrument flying and cross-country flying requirements.

The next step in getting a commercial license is to continue to log flying time and increase your knowledge and skills. To receive your commercial license you must be at least 18 years of age, have 250 hours of flying time, and successfully complete a number of exams. These tests include a physical exam; a written test given by the FAA covering such topics as safe flight operations, navigation principles, and federal aviation regulations; and a practical test to demonstrate your flying skills. Pilots must also receive a rating for the kind of plane they can fly (such as single-engine or multi-engine). In addition, a commercial pilot needs an instrument rating by the FAA and a restricted radio telephone operator's permit by the Federal

An agricultural pilot sprays pesticide on peas near Walla Walla, Washington. *(Doug Wilson, USDA)*

Communications Commission (FCC). In states where they spray restricted pesticides, agricultural pilots must be certified by the U.S. Department of Agriculture.

Other Requirements

All pilots must be of sound physical and emotional health. They need excellent eyesight and eye-hand coordination as well as excellent hearing and normal heart rate and blood pressure. The successful agricultural pilot is also detail-oriented since much paperwork, planning, and following of regulations is involved in this job. Those who are self-employed or working for smaller companies may find that they have frequent contact with customers, and so they must be able to work well with others. Naturally, an agricultural pilot should have an interest in farming methods and the environment as well as a love of flying. Good judgment is essential for this work.

EXPLORING

You can explore this field through a number of activities. Join groups such as your high school aviation club and the National FFA Organization (formerly Future Farmers of America). These groups may give you the opportunity to meet with professionals in the field, learn about farm products and management, and find others with similar interests. Read publications related to these industries such as the magazines *Agricultural Aviation* (http://www.agaviation.org /agmag.htm), *AgAir Update* (http://www.agairupdate.com), and *Progressive Farmer* (http://progressivefarmer.com). If you have the financial resources, you can take flying lessons once you are 16 and have passed a physical exam. Also, consider learning how to operate a ham radio. This skill will help you when you apply for your restricted radio operator's permit, a requirement for commercial pilots.

EMPLOYERS

California and the southern states, where the crop growing season lasts longest, are where agricultural pilots find the most work. They also find some work with northern crops and in forests of the northeastern and western states. Many are employed by crop-dusting companies, while others are self-employed. Federal and state government departments also employ agricultural pilots to assist with environmental, conservation, and preservation needs.

STARTING OUT

It is not unusual for people to enter this field after gaining experience in the agricultural industry itself, working on farms and learning about crop production while they also develop their flying skills. Others enter with flying as their first love and are drawn to the challenge of agricultural aviation. Once pilots have completed their training, they may find that contacts made through aviation schools lead to job openings. Those who have the financial means can begin by opening their own business. Equipment, however, is very expensive— a single plane appropriately outfitted can cost anywhere from $100,000 to $900,000. A number of people, therefore, begin by working for large aerial applications companies before they strike out on their own.

ADVANCEMENT

Agricultural pilots who work for a company can be promoted to manager. Self-employed agricultural pilots move up by charging more money for their services and increasing their client base. Another way to advance is to work in other areas of commercial aviation. These pilots may fly cargo and people to remote locations or become aerial photographers.

EARNINGS

If they work throughout the entire year, agricultural pilots can make between $30,000 and $80,000 per year. Those who fly about half the year make near $25,000. Agricultural pilots who are employed by companies rarely get paid vacation and only a few companies offer health and accident insurance and profit-sharing and pension plans.

WORK ENVIRONMENT

The vast majority of an agricultural pilot's job takes place outdoors, during the early morning and early evening hours. Their work is demanding and can be hazardous. When flying, agricultural pilots wear safety gear consisting of a helmet, safety belt, and shoulder harness, because they fly under such difficult conditions. They fly close to the ground in populated areas and must be cautious to avoid obstacles. They also face exposure to pesticides and other harsh substances. When mixing or loading chemicals onto the plane, they sometimes wear gloves or masks to prevent the inhaling of harmful vapors.

OUTLOOK

Employment opportunities for experienced agricultural pilots are expected to remain about the same for the next decade. However, the demand for agricultural pilots depends largely on farmers' needs. For example, during times when insect and pest control becomes a problem, there is greater demand for agricultural pilots. There is also some concern within the industry that genetically engineered crops (resistant to certain diseases) may decrease the need for aerial applications and cause a loss of business for agricultural pilots. Keeping these factors in mind, employment prospects will probably be best with larger farms and ranches and in states with long growing seasons.

FOR MORE INFORMATION

This organization has information on crop protection products and developments in the industry.
CropLife America
1156 Fifteenth Street, NW, Suite 400
Washington, DC 20005
Tel: 202-296-1585
http://www.acpa.org

This organization promotes high standards and continuing education in the field.

National Agricultural Aviation Association
1005 E Street, SE
Washington, DC 20003-2847
Tel: 202-546-5722
Email: information@agaviation.org
http://www.agaviation.org

For information on opportunities in the agricultural field and local chapters, contact

National FFA Organization
National FFA Center
6060 FFA Drive
PO Box 68960
Indianapolis, IN 46268-0960
Tel: 317-802-6060
http://www.ffa.org

Aircraft Mechanics

OVERVIEW

Aircraft mechanics examine, service, repair, and overhaul aircraft and aircraft engines. They also repair, replace, and assemble parts of the airframe (the structural parts of the plane other than the power plant or engine). There are about 154,000 aircraft mechanics working in the United States.

HISTORY

On December 17, 1903, Wilbur and Orville Wright made history's first successful powered flight. The Wright brothers—who originally built and repaired bicycles—designed, built, and repaired their airplane, including the engine, making them the first airplane mechanics as well. In the early years of aviation, most airplane designers filled a similar scope of functions, although many had people to assist them. As the aviation industry grew, the various tasks required to design, build, operate, and repair aircraft became more specialized. However, because of the instability of early planes and the uncertainty of the weather and other conditions, it was often necessary for pilots to have a strong working knowledge of how to repair and maintain their aircraft. In later years, one important route to becoming a pilot was to start as an aircraft mechanic.

As aircraft became capable of flying faster, for longer distances, and at higher altitudes, and especially after aircraft began to carry passengers, the role of the aircraft mechanic became vital to the safety of the aircraft and the growth of the aviation industry. New technologies have continually been introduced into the design of aircraft, and mechanics needed to be familiar with all the systems, from the airframe to the engine to the control systems. The complexity of airplane design increased to the point where the mechanics themselves began to specialize. Some mechanics had the skills to work on the entire aircraft. Others were able to work on the airframe, on the engines, or on the power plant. Some mechanics functioned as repairers, who completed minor repairs to the plane. Mechanics were assisted by technicians, who were often training to become fully qualified mechanics. With the introduction of electronics into aircraft, some mechanics specialized as avionics technicians.

The Air Commerce Act of 1926 imposed regulations on the commercial airlines and their fleets. The Federal Aviation Agency, later called the Federal Aviation Administration (FAA), also established training and licensing requirements for the mechanics servicing the airplanes. Mechanics were also an important part of the armed forces, especially during World War II, in which air power became a vital part of successful military operations.

The growth of the general aviation industry, which includes all flights operated outside of the airlines, provided still more demand for trained mechanics. The introduction of ultralight aircraft in the 1970s brought air flight back to its origins. These craft were often sold as kits that the purchasers had to build and repair themselves.

THE JOB

The work of aircraft mechanics employed by the commercial airlines may be classified into two categories: line maintenance mechanics and overhaul mechanics.

Line maintenance mechanics are all-around craft workers who make repairs on all parts of the plane. Working at the airport, they make emergency and other necessary repairs in the time between when aircraft land and when they take off again. They may be told by the pilot, flight engineer, or head mechanic what repairs need to be made, or they may thoroughly inspect the planes for oil leaks, cuts or dents in the surface and tires, or any malfunction in the radio, radar, and light equipment. In addition, their duties include changing oil, cleaning spark plugs, and replenishing the hydraulic and oxygen systems. They work as fast as safety permits so the aircraft can be put back into service quickly.

Overhaul mechanics keep the aircraft in top operating condition by performing scheduled maintenance, making repairs, and conducting inspections required by the FAA. Scheduled maintenance programs are based on the number of hours flown, calendar days, or a combination of these factors. Overhaul mechanics work at the airline's main overhaul base on either or both of the two major parts of the aircraft: the airframe, which includes wings, fuselage, tail assembly, landing gear, control cables, propeller assembly, and fuel and oil tanks; or the power plant, which may be a radial (internal combustion), turbojet, turboprop, or rocket engine.

Airframe mechanics work on parts of the aircraft other than the engine, inspecting the various components of the airframe for worn or defective parts. They check the sheet-metal surfaces, measure the tension of control cables, and check for rust, distortion, and cracks in the fuselage and wings. They consult manufacturers' manuals and the airline's maintenance manual for specifications and to determine whether repair or replacement is needed to correct defects or malfunctions. They also use specialized computer software to assist them in determining the need, extent, and nature of repairs. Airframe mechanics repair, replace, and assemble parts using a variety of tools, including power shears, sheet-metal breakers, arc and acetylene welding equipment, rivet guns, and air or electric drills.

Aircraft powerplant mechanics inspect, service, repair, and overhaul the engine of the aircraft. Looking through specially designed openings while working from ladders or scaffolds, they examine an engine's external appearance for such problems as cracked cylinders, oil leaks, or cracks or breaks in the turbine blades. They also listen to the engine in operation to detect sounds indicating malfunctioning components, such as sticking or burned valves. The test equipment used to check the engine's operation includes ignition analyzers, compression checkers, distributor timers, and ammeters. If necessary, the mechanics remove the engine from the aircraft, using a hoist or a forklift truck, and take the engine apart. They use sensitive instruments to measure parts for wear and use X-ray and magnetic inspection equipment to check for invisible cracks. Worn or damaged parts are replaced or repaired, then the mechanics reassemble and reinstall the engine.

Aircraft mechanics adjust and repair electrical wiring systems and aircraft accessories and instruments; inspect, service, and repair pneumatic and hydraulic systems; and handle various servicing tasks, such as flushing crankcases, cleaning screens, greasing moving parts, and checking brakes.

Mechanics may work on only one type of aircraft or on many different types, such as jets, propeller-driven planes, and helicopters. For greater efficiency, some specialize in one section, such as the electrical system, of a particular type of aircraft. Among the specialists, there are airplane electricians; pneumatic testers and pressure sealer-and-testers; aircraft body repairers and bonded

An aircraft mechanic rebuilds the engine of a small plane after engine problems grounded the aircraft. *(Mathew Hohmann)*

structures repairers, such as burnishers and bumpers; and air-conditioning mechanics, aircraft rigging and controls mechanics, plumbing and hydraulics mechanics, and experimental-aircraft testing mechanics. *Avionics technicians* are mechanics who specialize in the aircraft's electronic systems.

Mechanics who work for businesses that own their own aircraft usually handle all necessary repair and maintenance work. The planes, however, generally are small and the work is less complex than in repair shops.

In small, independent repair shops, mechanics must inspect and repair many different types of aircraft. The airplanes may include small commuter planes run by an aviation company, private company planes and jets, private individually owned aircraft, and planes used for flying instruction.

REQUIREMENTS

High School

The first requirement for prospective aircraft mechanics is a high school diploma. Courses in mathematics, physics, chemistry, and mechanical drawing are particularly helpful because they teach the principles involved in the operation of an aircraft, and this knowledge is often necessary to making the repairs. Machine shop, auto mechanics, or electrical shop are important courses for gaining many skills needed by aircraft mechanics.

Postsecondary Training

At one time, mechanics were able to acquire their skills through on-the-job training. This is rare today. Now most mechanics learn the job either in the armed forces or in trade schools approved by the FAA. The trade schools provide training with the necessary tools and equipment in programs that range in length from two years to 30 months. In considering applicants for certification, the FAA sometimes accepts successful completion of such schooling in place of work experience, but the schools do not guarantee an FAA certificate.

The experience acquired by aircraft mechanics in the armed forces sometimes satisfies the work requirements for FAA certification, and veterans may be able to pass the exam with a limited amount of additional study. But jobs in the military service are usually too specialized to satisfy the FAA requirement for broad work experience. In that case, veterans applying for FAA approval will have to complete a training program at a trade school. Schools occasionally give some credit for material learned in the service. However, on the plus side, airlines are especially eager to hire aircraft mechanics with both military experience and a trade school education.

Certification or Licensing

FAA certification is necessary for certain types of aircraft mechanics and is usually required to advance beyond entry-level positions. Most mechanics who work on civilian aircraft have FAA authorization as airframe mechanics, power plant mechanics, or avionics repair specialists. Airframe mechanics are qualified to work on the fuselage, wings, landing gear, and other structural parts of the aircraft; power plant mechanics are qualified for work on the engine. Mechanics may qualify for both airframe and power plant licensing, allowing them to work on any part of the plane. Combination airframe and power plant mechanics with an inspector's certificate are permitted to certify inspection work done by other mechanics. Mechanics without certification must be supervised by certified mechanics.

FAA certification is granted only to aircraft mechanics with previous work experience: a minimum of 18 months for an airframe or power plant certificate and at least 30 months working with both engines and airframes for a combination certificate. To qualify for an inspector's certificate, mechanics must have held a combined airframe and power plant certificate for at least three years. In addition, all applicants for certification must pass written and oral tests and demonstrate their ability to do the work authorized by the certificate.

Other Requirements

Aircraft mechanics must be able to work with precision and meet rigid standards. Their physical condition is also important. They need more than average strength for lifting heavy parts and tools, as well as agility for reaching and climbing. And they should not be afraid of heights, since they may work on top of the wings and fuselages of large jet planes.

In addition to education and certification, union membership may be a requirement for some jobs, particularly for mechanics employed by major airlines. The principal union organizing aircraft mechanics is the International Association of Machinists and Aerospace Workers. In addition, some mechanics are represented by the International Brotherhood of Teamsters, Chauffeurs, Warehousemen, and Helpers of America.

EXPLORING

Working with electronic kits, tinkering with automobile engines, and assembling model airplanes are good ways of gauging your ability to do the kinds of work performed by aircraft mechanics. A guided tour of an airfield can give you a brief overall view of this industry. Even better would be a part-time or summer job with an airline in an area such as the baggage department. Small airports may also offer job opportunities for part-time, summer, or replacement workers. You may also earn a student pilot license at the age of 16 and may gain more insight into the basic workings of an airplane that way. Kits for building ultralight craft are also available and may provide even more insight into the importance of proper maintenance and repair.

EMPLOYERS

Of the roughly 154,000 aircraft mechanics currently employed in the United States, about 60 percent work for air transportation companies and private maintenance and repair facilities. Each airline usually has one main overhaul base, where most of its mechanics are employed. These bases are found along the main airline routes or near large cities, including New York, Chicago, Los Angeles, Atlanta, San Francisco, and Miami.

Approximately 20 percent of aircraft mechanics works for the federal government. Many of these mechanics are civilians employed at military aviation installations, while others work for the FAA, mainly in its headquarters in Oklahoma City. About 13 percent work for aerospace products and parts manufacturing firms. Most of the rest are general aviation mechanics employed by independent repair shops at airports around the country, by businesses that use their own planes for transporting employees or cargo, by certified supplemental airlines, or by crop-dusting and air-taxi firms.

STARTING OUT

High school graduates who wish to become aircraft mechanics may enter this field by enrolling in an FAA-approved trade school. (Note that there are schools offering this training that do not have FAA approval.) These schools generally have placement services available for their graduates.

Another method is to make direct application to the employment offices of companies providing air transportation and services or the local offices of the state employment service, although airlines prefer to employ people who have already completed training. Many airports are managed by private fixed-base operators, which also operate the airport's repair and maintenance facilities. The field may also be entered through enlistment in the armed forces.

ADVANCEMENT

Promotions depend in part on the size of the organization for which an aircraft mechanic works. The first promotion after beginning employment is usually based on merit and comes in the form of a salary increase. To advance further, many companies require the mechanic to have a combined airframe and power plant certificate, or perhaps an aircraft inspector's certificate.

Advancement could take the following route: journeyworker mechanic, head mechanic or crew chief, inspector, head inspector, and shop supervisor. With additional training, a mechanic may advance to engineering, administrative, or executive positions. In larger airlines, mechanics may advance to become flight engineers, then copilots and pilots. With business training, some mechanics open their own repair shops.

EARNINGS

Although some aircraft mechanics, especially at the entry level and at small businesses, earn little more than the minimum wage, the median annual income for aircraft mechanics was about $43,077 in 2002, according to the U.S. Department of Labor. The middle 50 percent earned between $35,235 and $52,478. The bottom 10 percent earned less than $27,373. Experienced mechanics can earn more than $60,000 per year. Mechanics with airframe and powerplant certification earn more than those without it. Avionics technicians averaged $42,037 in 2002. Overtime, night shift, and holiday pay differentials are usually available and can greatly increase a mechanic's annual earnings.

Most major airlines are covered by union agreements. Their mechanics generally earn more than those working for other employers. Contracts usually include health insurance and often life insurance and retirement plans as well. An attractive fringe benefit for airline mechanics and their immediate families is free or reduced fares on their own and many other airlines. Mechanics working for the federal government also benefit from the greater job security of civil service and government jobs.

WORK ENVIRONMENT

Most aircraft mechanics work a five-day, 40-hour week. Their working hours, however, may be irregular and often include nights, weekends, and holidays, as airlines operate 24 hours a day, and extra work is required during holiday seasons.

When doing overhauling and major inspection work, aircraft mechanics generally work in hangars with adequate heat, ventilation, and lights. If the hangars are full, however, or if repairs must be made quickly, they may work outdoors, sometimes in unpleasant weather. Outdoor work is frequent for line maintenance mechanics, who work at airports, because they must make minor repairs and preflight checks at the terminal to save time. To maintain flight schedules, or to keep from inconveniencing customers in general aviation, the mechanics often have to work under time pressure.

The work is physically strenuous and demanding. Mechanics often have to lift or pull as much as 70 pounds of weight. They may stand, lie, or kneel in awkward positions, sometimes in precarious places such as on a scaffold or ladder.

Noise and vibration are common when testing engines. Regardless of the stresses and strains, aircraft mechanics are expected to work quickly and with great precision.

Although the power tools and test equipment are provided by the employer, mechanics may be expected to furnish their own hand tools.

OUTLOOK

The terrorist attacks of September 11, 2001, had a great impact on the aviation industry. Many airlines have reduced flights and cut back on workers. The outlook for aircraft mechanics, though, should improve over the course of the next decade. Employment opportunities will open up due to fewer young workers entering the labor force, fewer entrants from the military, and more retirees leaving positions. But the job prospects will vary according to the type of employer. Less competition for jobs is likely to be found at smaller commuter and regional airlines, FAA repair stations, and in general aviation. These employers pay lower wages and fewer applicants compete for their positions, while higher paying airline positions, which also include travel benefits, are more in demand among qualified applicants. Mechanics who keep up with technological advancements in electronics, composite materials, and other areas will be in greatest demand.

Employment of aircraft mechanics is likely to increase about as fast as the average through 2012, according to the U.S. Department of Labor. The demand for air travel and the numbers of aircraft created are expected to increase due to population growth and rising incomes. However, employment growth will be affected by the use of automated systems that make the aircraft mechanic's job more efficient. Slower-than-average employment growth is predicted for avionics technicians during this same time period.

FOR MORE INFORMATION

For career information, contact
Federal Aviation Administration
800 Independence Avenue, SW, Room 810
Washington, DC 20591
Tel: 202-366-4000
http://www.faa.gov/careers

For information on aviation maintenance and scholarships, contact
Professional Aviation Maintenance Association
717 Princess Street
Alexandria, VA 22314
Tel: 866-865-7262
Email: hq@pama.org
http://www.pama.org

Airplane Dispatchers

OVERVIEW

Airplane dispatchers plan and direct commercial air flights according to government and airline company regulations. They read radio reports from airplane pilots during flights and study weather reports to determine any necessary change in flight direction or altitude. They send instructions by radio to the pilots in the case of heavy storms, fog, mechanical difficulties, or other emergencies. Airline dispatchers are sometimes called *flight superintendents*.

HISTORY

Commercial air service took off slowly in the United States. The first airmail flight occurred in 1911. The first passenger air service was organized in 1914, providing air transportation from Tampa to St. Petersburg, Florida, but this service lasted only six months. In 1917, however, the U.S. Post Office began its first airmail service. In 1925, the Kelly Air Mail Act turned over the airmail routes to 12 private contractors. This formed the basis of the commercial airline industry in the United States.

The airline industry developed rapidly in the years leading up to World War II. The Air Commerce Act of 1927 introduced licensing requirements for pilots and airlines and created a network of defined airways. Improvements in airplane design had brought larger, more comfortable airplanes, and the numbers of passengers reached into the millions. By 1933, the United States boasted the busiest airports in the world.

These developments created a need for people to organize and guide the increasing numbers of flights operated by the airlines.

During the early days of aviation, the airplane dispatcher served in a number of capacities, including that of station manager, meteorologist, radio operator, and even mechanic. Often pilots were pressed into service as dispatchers because of their knowledge of weather and of the needs of flight crews. As the airline industry grew, these tasks became specialized. The first federal air traffic control center was opened in 1936. In 1938, federal licensing requirements were established for the airline's own dispatchers. Soon dispatchers were located all over the country.

Since that time, the work of dispatchers has become more involved and complicated, and the airline industry has relied on them extensively to make a major contribution to the safety of commercial air travel. Advancements in technology have eased parts of the airplane dispatcher's job and have also allowed the airlines to consolidate their remote dispatch offices to a smaller number of centrally located offices.

THE JOB

Airplane dispatchers are employed by commercial airlines, and they maintain a constant watch on factors affecting the movement of planes during flights. Dispatchers are responsible for the safety of flights and for making certain that they are operated on an efficient, profit-making basis. The work of dispatchers, however, is not the same as that of air traffic controllers, who are employees of the federal government.

Airplane dispatchers are responsible for giving the company's clearance for each flight that takes off during their shift. Their judgments are based on data received from a number of different sources. In their efforts to make certain that each flight will end successfully, they must take into consideration current weather conditions, weather forecasts, wind speed and direction, and other information. Before flights, they must decide whether the airplane crew should report to the field or whether the airline should begin notifying passengers that their flight has been delayed or canceled. Dispatchers may also have to determine whether an alternate route should be used, either to include another stop for passengers or to avoid certain weather conditions.

Upon reporting to the field before a flight, the pilot confers with the dispatcher and determines the best route to use, the amount of fuel to be placed aboard the aircraft, the altitude at which to fly, and the approximate flying time. The pilot and the dispatcher must agree on the conditions of the flight, and both have the option of delaying or canceling flights should conditions become too hazardous to ensure a safe trip.

Dispatchers may also be responsible for maintaining records and for determining the weight and balance of the aircraft after loading. They must be certain that all intended cargo is loaded aboard each of the appropriate flights. They must also be certain that all their decisions, such as those about the cargo, are in keeping with the safety regulations of the Federal Aviation Administration (FAA), as well as with the rules established by their own airline.

Once the planes are in the air, dispatchers keep in constant contact with the flight crews. A dispatcher may be responsible for communications with as many as 10 or 12 flights at any one time. Contact is maintained through a company-owned radio network that enables each company to keep track of all of its planes. Dispatchers keep the crews informed about the weather that they will encounter, and they record the positions and other information reported by the planes while they are en route. If an emergency occurs, dispatchers coordinate the actions taken in response to the emergency.

Following each flight, the pilot checks with the dispatcher for a debriefing. In the debriefing, the pilot brings the dispatcher up to date about the weather encountered in the air and other conditions related to the flight, so that the dispatcher will have this information available in scheduling subsequent flights.

Good judgment is an important tool of airplane dispatchers, for they must be able to make fast, workable, realistic decisions. Because of this, dispatchers often experience strains and tensions on the job, especially when many flights are in the air or when an emergency occurs.

In larger airlines, there is a certain degree of specialization among dispatchers. An assistant dispatcher may work with the chief dispatcher and have the major responsibility for just one phase of the dispatching activities, such as analyzing current weather information, while a senior dispatcher may be designated to take care of another phase, such as monitoring the operating costs of each flight.

REQUIREMENTS

High School

Some college education is required to be an airplane dispatcher, so if you are interested in this career you should follow a college prep curriculum. Business administration and computer skills are vital to the job, so take any courses available in those subjects. While in high school, you can also pursue a student pilot's license, which is a great advantage, though not a requirement.

Postsecondary Training
Airplane dispatchers are required to have at least two years of college education with studies in meteorology or air transportation. Two years of work experience in air transportation may take the place of the college requirement. Airlines prefer college graduates who have studied mathematics, physics, or meteorology.

There are a few schools around the country that offer dispatcher training. For information on these courses, contact the Airline Dispatchers Federation or visit its website at http://www.flightdispatch.net.

Certification or Licensing
Airplane dispatchers must be licensed by the FAA. You may prepare for the FAA licensing examination in several different ways. You may work at least one year in a dispatching office under a licensed dispatcher, complete an FAA-approved airline dispatcher's course at a specialized school or training center, or show that you have spent two of the previous three years in air traffic control work or a related job.

Candidates who meet the preliminary requirements must also pass an examination covering such subjects as civil air regulations, radio procedures, airport and airway traffic procedures, weather analysis, and air-navigation facilities. In addition to a written test, you must also pass an oral examination covering the interpretation of weather information, landing and cruising speeds of various aircraft, airline routes, navigation facilities, and operational characteristics of different types of aircraft. You must not only demonstrate your knowledge of these areas to become a licensed dispatcher, but you are also expected to maintain these skills once licensed. Various training programs, some of which may be conducted by employers, will assist you in staying current with new developments, which are frequent in this job.

Assistant dispatchers are not always required to be licensed. Thus, it may be possible to begin work in a dispatcher's office prior to earning the dispatcher's license.

Other Requirements
Airline dispatchers need to be able to work well either by themselves or with others and assume responsibility for their decisions. The job requires you to think and act quickly and sensibly under the most trying conditions. You may be responsible for hundreds of lives at any one time, and a poor decision could result in tragedy.

Airline dispatchers must be at least 23 years old and in good health. Your vision must be correctable to 20/20. A good memory, the ability to remain calm under great pressure and the ability to do many things at once, and to make decisions quickly are essential to a successful airplane dispatcher's career.

EXPLORING

Besides pursuing the course of study mentioned previously, there is little opportunity for an individual to explore the field of airplane dispatching directly. Part-time or summer jobs with airlines may provide interested students with a chance to observe some of the activities related to dispatching work. You can cultivate your interest in aircraft and aviation through reading and participating in flying clubs.

EMPLOYERS

The larger airlines employ only about 1,000 dispatchers. Smaller airlines and some private firms also employ airplane dispatchers, but the number of dispatchers remains very small. Virtually all airplane dispatchers are employed by commercial airlines, both those that ship cargo and those that transport passengers.

STARTING OUT

The occupation is not easy to enter because of its relatively small size and the special skills required. The nature of the training is such that it is not easily put to use outside of this specific area. Few people leave this career once they are in it, so only a few positions other than those caused by death or retirement become available.

People who are able to break into the field are often promoted to assistant dispatchers' jobs from related fields. They may come from among the airline's dispatch clerks, meteorologists, radio operators, or retired pilots. Obviously, airlines prefer those people who have had a long experience in ground-flight operations work. Thus, it is probably wise to plan on starting out in one of these related fields and eventually working into a position as an airplane dispatcher.

ADVANCEMENT

The usual path of advancement is from dispatch clerk to assistant dispatcher to dispatcher and then, possibly, to chief flight dispatcher or flight dispatch manager or assistant manager. It is also possible to become a chief flight supervisor or superintendent of flight control.

The line of advancement varies depending on the airline, the size of the facility where the dispatcher is located, and the positions available. At smaller facilities, there may be only two or three different promotional levels available.

EARNINGS

Dispatcher salaries vary greatly among airlines. According to the Airline Dispatchers Federation, entry-level positions at smaller carriers pay about $20,000 a year. Senior dispatchers at major airlines earn more than $100,000 a year. A few dispatchers earn close to $150,000 including overtime pay. Licensed dispatchers earn about $47,000 per year. Flight superintendents make up to about $52,800 per year, and shift chiefs, $66,000.

Airline positions generally provide health insurance and other benefits. Beginning dispatchers usually work eight-hour shifts five days a week and receive two weeks paid vacation per year. Senior dispatchers usually work four 10-hour shifts a week and may receive as many as six weeks vacation each year. Most dispatchers and their families are also able to fly for free or at heavily discounted prices.

WORK ENVIRONMENT

Airplane dispatchers are normally stationed at airports near a terminal or hangar, but in facilities away from the public. Some airlines use several dispatch installations, while others use a single office. Because dispatchers make decisions involving not only thousands of people but also a great deal of money, their offices are often located close to those of management, so that they can remain in close contact.

Frequently, the offices where airplane dispatchers work are full of noise and activity, with telephones ringing, computer printers chattering, and many people talking and moving about to consult charts and other sources of information. The offices usually operate 24 hours per day, with each dispatcher working eight-hour shifts, plus an additional half-hour used in briefing the relief person.

Many lives depend on airplane dispatchers every day. This means that there is often considerable stress in their jobs. Dispatchers must constantly make rapid decisions based on their evaluation of a great deal of information. Adding to the tension is the fact that they may work in noisy, hectic surroundings and must interact with many people throughout the day. However, dispatchers can feel deep satisfaction in knowing that their job is vital to the safety and success of airline operations.

OUTLOOK

The Airline Dispatchers Federation (ADF) says the job market for dispatchers is currently good, especially with smaller commuter airlines. However, the centralization of dispatch offices using more advanced technology means that fewer dispatchers will be able to do more work. With improved communications equipment, a single dispatcher will be able to cover a larger area than is currently possible. Because of the relatively small size of this occupational field, its employment outlook is not particularly good.

Most major airlines consider dispatch positions as senior management positions. Candidates are often selected from within the company after they have accumulated 15 to 20 years of experience in a variety of areas, including supervisory positions. Candidates selected from outside the company must have considerable experience with smaller carriers.

According to ADF, new graduates from dispatch schools should not expect to be hired by major airlines such as American or United. A better choice would be to seek a position with a smaller carrier and get at least five years' experience before attempting to apply for a position with a major airline.

FOR MORE INFORMATION

For career information, contact
Airline Dispatchers Federation
2020 Pennsylvania Avenue, NW, #821
Washington, DC 20006
Tel: 800-676-3685
http://www.flightdispatch.net

For information on training, contact
Airline Flight Dispatcher Training Center
4501 Highway 360 South/Falcon Wing, Suite 203 MD929
Fort Worth, TX 76155
Tel: 817-967-4424
Email: afdtc1@hotmail.com
http://www.airlinedispatcher.com

For information on aviation careers, contact
Federal Aviation Administration
800 Independence Avenue, SW, Room 810
Washington, DC 20591
Tel: 202-366-4000
http://www.faa.gov/careers

Airport Security Personnel

OVERVIEW

Airport security personnel is a blanket term describing all workers who protect the safety of passengers and staff in the nation's airports and aircraft. One of the largest group of personnel in this line of work is *security screeners,* who are responsible for identifying dangerous objects or hazardous materials in baggage, cargo, or on traveling passengers and preventing these objects and their carriers from boarding planes. Also included in this group of workers are *air marshals,* who act as on-board security agents, protecting passengers, pilots, and other airline staff in the case of any emergencies while in the air. More than 40,000 people are employed in airport security.

HISTORY

The use of screening and onboard security personnel is not a recent invention. The presence of guards on airplanes originated in the 1960s as a result of a number of hijackings of U.S. planes flying to and from Cuba. These guards, referred to as Sky Marshals, grew in number during the 1970s and then declined in later years with the lower occurrences of airplane hijackings. Airplane security staffing reached several thousand workers at the peak of this hijacking scare, then dropped to fewer than 100 workers nationwide during its quietest times.

Airport security workers monitor security conditions using remote cameras and video screens. *(Photo Disc)*

The 2001 terrorist attacks on the World Trade Center and the Pentagon spurred many changes in the realm of airport security. Most notably, a new federal agency was born: the Transportation Security Administration (TSA), responsible for overseeing all security at the nation's airports. This agency made airport and airline security a federal responsibility, and as a result, all airport security personnel became federal employees. This was no small task. Previously, security screening in airports was handled by private security firms. These firms were inconsistent in their hiring and training methods and paid relatively low wages—resulting in high job turnover rates and inadequate screening of potentially dangerous objects and materials. With the shift of responsibility into the government's hands, standard training and hiring requirements were put in place. In addition to better screening, hiring, and training methods, the technology for screening bags and passengers has improved, increasing the chances that dangerous cargo and on-person threats can be located and prevented from boarding a plane.

THE JOB

Protecting U.S. skies, airports, and passengers is a huge undertaking that requires many qualified, well-trained individuals in different security roles. The most visible airport security worker is the security screener, also called the *baggage and passenger screener*. These workers use computers, X-ray machines, and handheld scanners to screen bags and their owners passing through airport terminals. In addition to using technology to help them identify dangerous items, they also have to depend on their own eyesight to catch suspicious behavior and read the X-ray screens for signs of danger. These workers must be focused and alert, while also remaining personable and courteous to people being screened. The screening process can take a lot of time during high-volume travel days, and passengers waiting in line may be late for a flight, impatient, or simply rude. For this reason, security screeners must be people-oriented, able to manage crowds, and maintain composure in what can be stressful conditions.

The need for security is not limited to the ground. Air marshals, also called *security agents,* have the demanding job of protecting all airline passengers and staff from on-board threats, such as terrorists, hijackers, bombs, or other weapons. These workers are often covert in their operations, meaning they may be dressed and seated like an average passenger to be able to watch for suspicious behavior and surprise a potential attacker. Much of the details of air marshal jobs are classified to protect national security, such as their exact number and identities, routes, and training procedures. However the basics of their job is much like that of a Secret Service agent. They must be attentive to all activity that goes on around them, identify potential threats to security, and deal with dangerous individuals or objects once exposed on board. The main difference between air marshals and other security agents is they must be trained and able to handle possible warfare in a confined space at 30,000 feet in the air.

Another airport security job of high importance is that of *security director*. These workers, hired by the federal government, are responsible for all security personnel within an airport. They oversee the hiring, training, and work of baggage and passenger screeners, air marshals, and other security guards. In the nation's largest airports, such as JFK in New York City or O'Hare in Chicago, directors are in charge of hundreds of workers. Because of the high level of responsibility held by these workers, security directors often have previous experience in crisis management or law enforcement, such as police chiefs or military officers.

REQUIREMENTS

High School

To work in most airport security jobs, you should have at least a high school diploma. However, security screeners can sidestep this educational requirement with previous job experience in security. While in high school, take classes in history and government to familiarize yourself with previous events and political threats that have threatened our national security, such as foreign hijackers and terrorist operations. You should also be comfortable working with computers since most jobs in security involve a great deal of technology. Math classes can be beneficial because as a security worker, you must be analytical and observant to identify and catch dangers before they happen.

Postsecondary Training

All security workers, from screeners to directors, are highly trained before starting their jobs. Screeners are trained on how to operate and identify dangerous objects from the X-ray machines and handheld wands. They also must be prepared to manage potentially dangerous individuals. Screeners currently receive 40 hours of training before their first day at work, and receive an additional 60 hours of training while on the job. This training period may be extended due to increased scrutiny on screeners' performance and heightened national security risks.

Air marshals are rigorously trained in classified training centers across the country, and they come to the job with previous on-the-job experience from serving in a military or civilian police force. Similarly, security directors must have previous federal security experience and are trained for up to 400 hours before taking onthe responsibility of directing an entire airport security staff.

Other Requirements

All airport security personnel have demanding jobs that require a calm demeanor when under pressure. Screeners often have to stand for hours at a time and assist in lifting passengers' luggage onto the screening belt. Their eyesight must be strong enough to detect even the smallest of possible threats displayed on a computer screen. To ensure that individuals can handle these demands, potential screeners face many physical and vision tests to ensure they are up to the job. All screeners must be U.S. citizens or nationals and pass tests evaluating mental abilities (English reading, writing, and speaking), visual observation (including color perception), hearing, and manual dexterity. Similarly, air marshals and directors of security must pass vision and hearing tests and be in good physical shape to face and dominate potential attackers.

EXPLORING

To explore this job, watch people at work your next time at the airport. Notice how many people are involved in screening luggage and passengers. While you should not talk to these screeners and other security staff while they are at work, you may be able to schedule an interview with security personnel while they are on break or perhaps over the phone. Talk to a teacher or your school's guidance counselor for help in arranging this.

You can also learn about security jobs at your local library or online. Explore the websites of the Federal Aviation Administration (FAA) for facts and job descriptions, changes in policy, and even summer camp opportunities. The links at the end of this article are good places to start your research.

EMPLOYERS

In late 2001, airport and airline security was placed under the oversight of the federal government. While some screening jobs may still be handled by private companies, all security personnel are screened and trained under federal rules and regulations. This shift in responsibility was done to improve standards in security and ensure the safety of U.S. passengers and airline staff. The newly created Transportation Security Administration (TSA) and the FAA are the employers of all airport security staff. There are more than 40,000 people employed in airport security, approximately 28,000 of whom are security screeners working in the nation's airports.

STARTING OUT

Depending on the security level you want to be employed in, you can start out working with no more than a high school diploma and on-the-job training. Security screening jobs are a great way to start out in this line of work. These jobs provide front-line experience in airport security and can offer flexible part-time schedules.

Positions as air marshals or directors or security are not entry-level positions. If you are interested in one of these jobs, you will need previous experience with the police, U.S. military, or other position in which you have gained skills in protecting the lives of others.

ADVANCEMENT

Screening jobs have high turnover rates and, as a result, offer many chances for advancement. After a couple of years of experience in baggage and passenger screening, you can work into higher positions in management or busier traffic responsibility. Security managers may be responsible for hundreds of workers and oversee the hiring and training of new workers.

Positions as air marshals already offer a high level of responsibility, but qualified and talented individuals can advance into manager and director roles, responsible for hundreds and even thousands of workers.

EARNINGS

Before airline security was adopted by the TSA, screeners were paid minimum wage. But to attract and retain qualified and dedicated workers, earnings have been raised considerably, with most full-time screeners earning salaries of $30,000 to $35,000 a year. Their pay increases as their level of experience and responsibility increases. Air marshals and directors earn much more, with directors topping out at a salary of $150,000 or more—one of the highest salaries in government service.

WORK ENVIRONMENT

As previously stated, any job in airport security is demanding and stressful, especially during high periods of travel, such as the holidays. Screeners face physical challenges of standing, bending, and lifting during their shifts, while having to maintain total visual focus on their X-ray machines or while searching individual passengers by hand.

The job of air marshals can be extremely stressful. These workers must be prepared to overcome an attacker in a confined space without risking harm to any of the plane's passengers. In addition, air marshals must spend considerable time away from home.

OUTLOOK

With the new awareness of airline dangers following recent terrorist attacks, the employment of airport security personnel will grow at a faster-than-average rate. Despite better pay, security screeners still have high turnover rates due to the high demands involved with the job. This turnover will continue to create many new jobs in the future. While jobs as air marshals and security directors will not be as plentiful, there will always be a critical need for qualified and skilled individuals to protect airplanes and passengers from security threats.

FOR MORE INFORMATION

The FAA offers a wealth of information on its website, from airline accident statistics to career guidance. Visit the Education pages for information on summer camps for middle and high school students interested in aviation careers.

Federal Aviation Administration
800 Independence Avenue, SW
Washington, DC 20591
Tel: 202-366-4000
http://www.faa.gov

According to its website, the TSA "sets the standard for excellence in transportation security through its people, processes, and technologies." Explore the site for details on the nation's threat advisory level and tips on flying and packing safely.

Transportation Security Administration
TSA-21 Human Resources
601 South 12th Street
Arlington, VA 22202-4220
http://www.tsa.gov

Airport Service Workers

QUICK FACTS

School Subjects
Business
Family and consumer science
Speech

Personal Skills
Following instructions
Mechanical/manipulative

Work Environment
Indoors and outdoors
Primarily multiple locations

Minimum Education Level
High school diploma

Salary Range
$10,712 to $20,800 to
$100,000

Certification or Licensing
Required for certain
positions

Outlook
About as fast as the average

DOT
005, 157, 185, 290, 310,
311, 313, 319, 382, 408,
824, 912

(continues)

OVERVIEW

The term *airport service worker* is a general designation for a wide variety of workers who are employed in support occupations at airports. Many of these workers deal directly with the public in sales- and service-based occupations. Others perform behind-the-scenes maintenance and cleaning services that keep public and private areas of airports clean and operating efficiently.

HISTORY

In the early days of aviation, there were no airports as we know them today. Planes landed on flat strips of dirt and grass, and there were few, if any, services available for passengers. By the 1930s, the first airports were constructed in New York, Chicago, and other major cities. But it was not until after World War II that commercial air travel began to really take off and services began to be offered to make travel easier and more convenient for airline passengers. Large numbers of airport service workers were hired to staff airport restaurants and shops, keep facilities clean, and assist travelers with baggage and general information. Today, these workers serve over 30 million travelers annually at approximately 540 commercial services airports in the United States.

THE JOB

Airport service workers perform a variety of duties that are integral to the proper functioning of an airport. The following paragraphs detail some of the major airport service careers.

Airport parking attendants sell parking tickets, collect payments, and direct cars into the proper parking spaces. Many airports offer transportation from remote parking lots to the terminals. *Airport drivers* operate trolley cars, trams, buses, vans, and trains and give general assistance to passengers. Some airport drivers operate airfield vehicles such as food trucks, employee buses, fuel trucks, and other equipment.

Skycaps, also known as *baggage porters,* help customers with luggage at airports. They are either employed by airlines or by ground services companies. Skycaps stand at curbside airline entrances and help travelers load and unload baggage, answer questions about flight schedules, and often check in luggage.

Airport concession workers are employed at gift shops, bookstores, car rental agencies, newsstands, and any other place goods or services are sold. Besides making and completing cash and credit card sales, attendants are responsible for stocking and pricing items, helping customers with their purchases, and answering any questions regarding the merchandise or services. Attendants also make sure displays are clean and orderly.

Airport food concession attendants sell snacks and beverages to travelers at small airport kiosks. Attendants are trained on the proper way to prepare and serve their snacks and make cash and credit card transactions as well.

Airport food service workers are employed in eating establishments at airports. *Waiters* and *waitresses* take customers' orders, serve food and beverages, calculate bills, and sometimes collect money. Between serving customers, waiters may clear and clean tables and counters, replenish supplies, and set up table service for future customers. *Cooks* and *chefs* are employed in the preparation and cooking of food in restaurants and other eating establishments. *Fast food workers* take food and drink orders from customers. During quiet periods, they may

QUICK FACTS

(continued)

GOE
03.01.03, 05.01.07,
05.05.05, 05.09.03,
05.10.08, 05.12.06,
05.12.18, 09.01.03,
09.04.01, 09.04.02,
09.05.02, 11.11.05

NOC
0621, 0631, 2225, 6211,
6241, 6242, 6421, 6452,
6641, 6661, 6663

O*NET-SOC
11-9051.00, 35-1011.00,
35-1012.00, 35-2011.00,
35-2014.00, 35-2015.00,
35-2021.00, 35-3011.00,
35-3021.00, 35-3022.00,
35-3031.00, 35-9011.00,
35-9021.00, 37-1011.02,
37-1012.00, 37-2011.00,
37-3011.00, 39-6011.00,
41-1011.00, 41-2011.00,
41-2031.00

be responsible for such chores as making coffee, cooking french fries, or cleaning tables. *Bartenders* mix and dispense alcoholic and nonalcoholic drinks in airport restaurants and bars.

Restaurant and food service managers are responsible for the overall operation of airport businesses that serve food. Food service work includes the purchasing of a variety of food, selection of the menu, preparation of the food, and, most importantly, maintenance of health and sanitation levels. It is the responsibility of managers to oversee staffing for each task in addition to performing the business and accounting functions of restaurant operations.

Some airport food service workers are employed by the airlines or private contractors to prepare and cook food that is consumed during flights. They work in airport flight kitchens. Other food service employees in airports include bar backs, buspersons, dishwashers, and kitchen assistants.

Airport janitors or *cleaners* clean and maintain all areas of the airport, including terminals, washrooms, security areas, shops, restaurants, bars, waiting areas, and offices. In addition to daily cleaning duties, they may perform light repair work when needed and make sure heating and cooling systems are in proper working order. Larger airports employ separate tradesworkers, such as carpenters, electricians, plumbers, and building engineers, to repair and maintain airport facilities.

Groundsmanagers and *groundskeepers* oversee the maintenance of land and vegetation at airports and their surrounding facilities.

Airport information specialists assist passengers in airport terminals. They answer general questions and help disabled passengers. Some airport information specialists work as translators and help foreign travelers.

REQUIREMENTS

High School

While most airport service positions are available to high school students, the most attractive positions will go to high school graduates. In high school, take courses in mathematics, business, and computer science to prepare for work in these careers. English and speech classes will help you to develop your communication skills, and a foreign language will help you to interact with foreign travelers.

Postsecondary Training

Most airport service positions are open to high school students. They learn the duties and responsibilities of their specific position via on-the-job training. Other airport service workers prepare for their careers by enrolling in postsecondary training programs. For example, cooks and chefs may pursue additional education at private vocational schools or university programs. They may also participate in apprenticeship programs that are sponsored by professional associations and trade unions. To improve their management abilities and increase their chances of promotion, many food service managers earn an associate's or bachelor's degree in restaurant management or institutional food service management. Airport tradesworkers, such as carpenters, electricians, plumbers, and building engineers, usually learn their respective trade by participating in an apprenticeship program or attending a technical or vocational educational program.

Certification and Licensing
Certification and licensing requirements vary based on the type of airport service career. The following paragraphs detail certification and licensing requirements for selected airport service careers.

Applicants who pass an examination can receive the certified parking facility manager designation from the National Parking Association.

In most states, airport and other professional drivers must qualify for a commercial driver's license. State motor vehicle departments can provide information on how to qualify for this license. For insurance reasons, companies generally prefer to hire drivers who are at least 25 years of age and have an impeccable driving record.

Chefs, cooks, and other food service workers are required by law in most states to possess a health certificate and to be examined periodically. These examinations, usually given by the state board of health, make certain that the individual is free from communicable diseases and skin infections. The National Restaurant Association Educational Foundation offers a voluntary foodservice management professional certification to restaurant and food service managers.

Although not a requirement for finding a job, some janitors opt to become certified by the National Executive Housekeepers Association.

Groundsmanagers and groundskeepers can receive voluntary certification from several organizations, including the Associated Landscape Contractors of America, the Professional Grounds Management Society, and the Professional Lawn Care Association of America.

Aviation Facts

- The Boeing 247 was the first modern passenger airliner. It was introduced in 1933.

- The first pressurized aircraft, the Stratoliner, was introduced in 1940.

- The Tupolev 144 was the first supersonic commercial aircraft. It was built by the Soviet Union in 1968.

- The first widebody jet, the Boeing 747, was built in 1969. It had two aisles, an upper deck, four engines, and seating for up to 450 passengers.

- Commercial air travel in the United States is safer than travel on its highways. More than 40,000 people die a year in highway accidents. In 1974, the worst year of aviation accidents, 460 people lost their lives.

- There are 544 commercial service airports in the United States.

Source: Air Transport Association of America

Other Requirements

Airport service workers who deal with the public must have strong communication skills, pleasant personal appearances, tact, patience, and the ability to interact with a wide range of people. All workers must be able to follow instructions and have good physical stamina to stand for long periods of time. Workers who are employed in sales occupations must be able to add and subtract accurately and quickly and operate cash registers and other types of business machines.

Skycaps must have physical strength to lift heavy luggage and excellent communication skills to deal with customers effectively. Airport drivers must have a good driving record and be able drive in all types of weather conditions.

Bartenders must be at least 21 years of age, although some employers prefer they be older than 25. In some states, bartenders must have health certificates assuring that they are free of contagious diseases. Because of the large sums of money collected in some bars, bartenders must sometimes be bonded.

Janitors and tradesworkers should be good with their hands and be able to operate tools and equipment. A certain level of stamina and energy is essential since the job requires physical labor.

Groundskeepers must be able to follow directions and be responsible, since they are often assigned duties and then asked to work without direct supervision.

Information specialists must have excellent communication skills and an encyclopedic knowledge of airport services and facilities in order to quickly and effectively serve the needs of travelers.

EXPLORING

One way to learn more about these careers is to visit an airport and watch these workers as they do their jobs. You might also ask your guidance counselor or teacher to set up an information interview with a worker in the field. You can also try to get a part-time or summer job at an airport as a food service worker, shop clerk, janitor, information specialist, or other service worker.

EMPLOYERS

Airport service workers are employed at the approximately 540 commercial services airports in the United States. Some work directly for airlines, while others work for private contractors. Additionally, almost all of these positions can be found outside of airports. For example, skycaps are also employed in bus terminals, train stations, cruise ships, and just about any place of travel. Skycaps known as *baggage porters* and *bellhops* assist guests at hotels and motels. Food service workers are employed by hotels, bars, restaurants, and schools. Janitors and cleaners work in hotels, restaurants, offices, schools, malls, stadiums, and in countless other settings. Grounds workers are employed at golf and country clubs, public parks and recreation areas, apartment complexes, cemeteries, condominiums, estates, schools and universities, shopping centers and malls, theme parks, zoos, commercial and industrial parks, hospitals, and military installations. Information specialists can also be employed at rail and bus stations, amusement parks, shopping malls, trade shows, concert halls, and sports stadiums.

STARTING OUT

Airport service careers represent an excellent way to break into the aviation industry at the ground level. Contact your local airport authority for a list of concession contractors to which you can apply for employment directly.

ADVANCEMENT

With hard work, dedication, and additional education or training, airport service workers can advance to a variety of managerial and supervisory positions. For example, food service workers can become chefs or food service managers. Experienced janitors and cleaners may be asked to supervise large groups of workers. Those with experience, contacts, references, and an interest in entrepreneurship could start their own businesses.

EARNINGS

Salaries for airport service workers vary based on the size and location of the airport and the worker's job description and level of experience. Airport drivers earn approximately $7 to $8 an hour. Skycaps earn salaries that range from $13,200 to $25,200 plus tips, according to the FAA. According to CNN.com, experienced skycaps can earn between $75,000 and $100,000 a year. Airport concession workers earn salaries that range from minimum wage to approximately $10 per hour. Food preparers earn $6 to $9 an hour. Food service managers employed in scheduled air transportation earned mean annual salaries of $64,100 in 2002, according to the U.S. Department of Labor. Janitors and cleaners employed in scheduled air transportation had mean annual salaries of $29,680 in 2002.

WORK ENVIRONMENT

With millions of travelers from countless states and countries passing through annually, airports are hectic but exciting places to work. And like the diverse travelers they serve, airport service workers enjoy a wide variety of work environments. Workers employed in concessions and food service work indoors in a comfortable, climate-controlled environment. Others, such as janitors and cleaners and maintenance staff, work both indoors and outdoors to keep airport facilities maintained. Skycaps spend most of their workday outdoors on their feet in sometimes severe weather conditions. Airport drivers work in all types of weather conditions. They are constantly on the go, transporting passengers, airport employees, and equipment and goods to various locations. Groundsmanagers and groundskeeping crews work outside year-round in all types and conditions of weather. Grounds workers frequently use pesticides, herbicides, and fungicides to keep turf, plants, shrubs, trees, and flowers healthy and beautiful. It is essential that they observe safety precautions when applying these chemicals to prevent exposure.

Since most airports are open 24 hours a day, seven days a week, airport service workers may be required to work nights and on weekends.

OUTLOOK

Employment in the air transportation industry is expected to grow more slowly than the average for all industries through 2012, according to the *Career Guide to Industries.* As a result of reduced passenger travel in recent years, there have been many layoffs and some airlines and other aviation-related companies went bankrupt. The U.S. Department of Labor predicts that the industry will gradually bounce back as the public regains confidence in flying as a result of post-9/11 security measures and business travel increases as the nation's economy improves and world trade expands. Of course, another terrorist attack or even the threat of an attack will greatly affect the employment of airport service workers. If the public travels less, there will be less demand for service and support workers at airports. Certain positions will be hit especially hard. For example, during heightened security alerts, curbside check-in is banned, which affects employment for skycaps.

Overall, there should be many job openings for workers in this field since these positions pay relatively low salaries and require little educational preparation. Positions will become available as workers leave the field for better-paying positions with more opportunity for advancement.

FOR MORE INFORMATION

To read The Airline Handbook, *visit the ATAA website.*
Air Transport Association of America
1301 Pennsylvania Avenue, NW, Suite 1100
Washington, DC 20004-1707
Tel: 202-626-4000
Email: ata@airlines.org
http://www.airlines.org

For information on careers and training in the janitorial services field, contact
Cleaning and Maintenance Management Online
National Trade Publications
13 Century Hill Drive
Latham, NY 12110
Tel: 518-783-1281
http://www.cmmonline.com

For general information on aviation, contact
Federal Aviation Administration
800 Independence Avenue, SW, Room 810
Washington, DC 20591
Tel: 202-366-4000
http://www.faa.gov

For information on educational programs, contact
**International Council on Hotel, Restaurant and Institutional
    Education**
2613 North Parham Road, 2nd Floor
Richmond, VA 23294
Tel: 804-346-4800
Email: info@chrie.org
http://chrie.org

For information about certification programs in housekeeping, contact
**International Executive Housekeepers
    Association Inc.**
1001 Eastwind Drive, Suite 301
Westerville, OH 43081-3361
Tel: 800-200-6342
Email: excel@ieha.org
http://www.ieha.org

*For information on certification for parking facility managers,
contact*
National Parking Association
1112 16th Street, NW, Suite 300
Washington, DC 20036
Tel: 800-647-PARK
Email: info@npapark.org
http://www.npapark.org

For information on education, scholarships, and careers, contact
**National Restaurant Association
    Educational Foundation**
175 West Jackson Boulevard, Suite 1500
Chicago, IL 60604-2702
Tel: 800-765-2122
Email: info@foodtrain.org
http://www.nraef.org

For materials on educational programs in the retail industry, contact
National Retail Federation
325 7th Street, NW, Suite 1100
Washington, DC 20004
Tel: 800-673-4692
http://www.nrf.com

For information on student membership and certification, contact
Professional Grounds Management Society
720 Light Street
Baltimore, MD 21230 ˎ
Tel: 410-752-3318
Email: pgms@assnhqtrs.com
http://www.pgms.org

Air Traffic Controllers

QUICK FACTS

School Subjects
Computer science
Geography

Personal Skills
Leadership/management
Technical/scientific

Work Environment
Primarily indoors
Primarily one location

Minimum Education Level
High school diploma

Salary Range
$29,821 to $95,700 to
$150,000

Certification or Licensing
Required by all states

Outlook
About as fast as the average

DOT
193

GOE
05.03.03

NOC
2272

O*NET-SOC
53-2021.00

OVERVIEW

Air traffic controllers monitor and direct the activities of aircraft into and out of airports and along specified flight routes. They radio pilots with approach, landing, taxiing, and takeoff instructions and advisories on weather and other conditions. These reports help maintain the safe and orderly flow of air traffic both in the air and on the ground. There are approximately 26,000 air traffic controllers employed in the United States.

HISTORY

The goal of the first air traffic control efforts—beacon lights—was to guide airplanes along a specified airway. As airways and aircraft grew in number, radio communication and radio beacons were added to help planes navigate and to provide weather forecasts. In 1936, the federal government opened the first air traffic control center to regulate the increasing numbers of aircraft flying into and out of the country's growing airports. The Instrument Landing System, a method for signaling aircraft, was instituted in 1941. Airplanes were reaching higher speeds and altitudes, and the controllers' functions became more important to guard against collisions, to ensure safe landings, and to warn pilots of potential weather and geographic hazards in flights. Radar, developed during World War II, allowed air traffic controllers to track the movements of many aircraft and for longer distances. The air traffic control network was extended to include centers at airports, en route centers, and flight service stations, each of which performed specific tasks and controlled specific portions of the skies. After the war, more sophisticated communication systems were developed, including VOR (very high frequency omni-directional range) transmission, which was used to signal flight path data directly to the plane. Computers were soon installed in order to provide still greater accuracy to the air traffic controller's instructions. Development of the Global Positioning System (GPS), however, has made it possible for airplanes to achieve greater control over their flight paths, so fewer air traffic controllers will be needed to protect the skies.

THE JOB

Air traffic controllers work in one of three areas: airport traffic control towers, en route air traffic control centers, or flight service stations. The Federal Aviation Administration (FAA), which regulates all air traffic, employs almost every air traffic controller in the United States. Some private airports employ their own air traffic controllers; others are employed at military airports.

Terminal air traffic control specialists are stationed in airport control towers and are responsible for all air traffic entering, leaving, or passing through the airspace around the airport, as well as conducting airplane traffic on the ground. These controllers use radar and visual observation to maintain safe distances among aircraft, and they provide information on weather and other conditions to the pilots under their control. As an airplane prepares for departure, the *ground controller* issues taxiing instructions to bring it to the runway. A *local controller* contacts the pilot with weather, wind, speed, and visibility conditions and clears the pilot for takeoff. A *departure controller* monitors the aircraft on radar, maintains radio contact with the pilot until the aircraft has left the airport's airspace, and hands over control of the plane to an en route control center. A *radar controller* monitors the traffic above the airport and into the aircraft's flight route, communicating with the other controllers. Approaching aircraft are handled in a reverse procedure. When many aircraft are approaching the airport at the same time, the controllers arrange them in a holding pattern above the airport until they each can be cleared to land.

There are more than 440 air traffic control towers in airports across the country. At a small airport, an air traffic controller may be expected to perform all of these functions. Controllers at larger airports usually specialize in a single area. *Senior controllers* supervise the activities of the entire center. *Terminal air traffic controllers* may be responsible for all aircraft within as much as a 50-mile radius of their airport. Most controllers are responsible for many aircraft at once; they track their positions on the radar screen, receive instrument flight data such as an airplane's speed and altitude, coordinate the altitudes at which planes within the area will fly, keep track of weather conditions, and maintain constant communication with the pilots and with controllers at their and other control centers. An air traffic controller must be aware of all of the activities in the air traffic control center and around the airport. When an aircraft experiences an emergency, air traffic controllers must respond quickly, clearing a path for that aircraft through the traffic, alerting fire and rescue teams, and guiding the pilot to a safe landing.

En route air traffic control specialists work at one of 21 regional centers in the United States. They coordinate the movements of aircraft between airports but out of range of the airport traffic controllers. Because an en route center may be responsible for many thousands of square miles of airspace, these controllers generally work in teams of two or three, with each team assigned a particular section of the center's airspace. Each team consists of a radar controller, the senior member of the team, and radar associates. A center may employ as many as 700 controllers and have 150 or more on duty during peak flying hours. Within the center's airspace are designated routes that the aircraft fly. En route controllers monitor traffic along those air routes. They use radar and electronic equipment to track the flights within the center's airspace and to maintain contact with planes within their area, giving instructions, air traffic clearances, and advice about flight conditions. If flight plans for two airplanes conflict, the en route team will contact the team responsible for the preceding section in order to change one plane's flight path. The controllers will also coordinate changes in altitudes and speeds among pilots. En route controllers receive or transfer control of the aircraft to controllers in adjacent centers or to an airport's approach controller as the craft enters that facility's airspace.

Flight service station air traffic control specialists make up the third group of controllers. They provide preflight or inflight assistance to pilots from more than 125 flight service stations linked by a communications system. These controllers give pilots information about the station's particular area, including terrain, weather, and anything else necessary to guarantee a safe flight. They may suggest alternate routes or different altitudes, alert pilots to military operations taking place along certain routes, inform them about landing at airports that have no towers, assist pilots in emergency situations, and participate in searches for missing or overdue aircraft.

REQUIREMENTS

High School

Because it is highly recommended for all air traffic controllers to have a college degree, high school students interested in the field will be best prepared by pursuing a college prep curriculum. Mathematics and science courses are most directly related to air traffic control work.

Postsecondary Training

To become an air traffic controller, a person must enroll in one of 14 education programs recognized by the FAA. They must also pass a preemployment test that gauges their aptitude for the career and have completed four years of college or have three years of work experience or a combination of both. Entry to civil aviation is also possible through the military.

Those accepted into the training program receive 12 weeks of intensive instruction at the FAA Academy in Oklahoma City. There they receive training in the fundamentals of the airway systems, civil air regulations, radar, and aircraft performance characteristics. They practice on machines designed to simulate emergency situations to determine their emotional stability under pressure. The standards for those who successfully complete this program are very high; about 50 percent of the trainees are dropped during this period. Those who complete the program are guaranteed jobs with the FAA.

Certification or Licensing

Training continues on the job, and new controllers also receive classroom instruction. Depending on the size and complexity of the facility, a new hire may require between 18 months and three years to become a fully certified air traffic controller. Controllers must be certified at each progressive level of air traffic control, usually within a certain period of time. Failure to be certified within the time limit is grounds for dismissal. Air traffic controllers are also required to pass annual physical exams and performance reviews.

Other Requirements

Applicants for airport tower or en route traffic control jobs must be 30 years of age or younger, pass physical and psychological examinations, be U.S. citizens, and have vision that is or can be corrected to 20/20. Flight service stations will accept applicants who are over the age of 30. Those hoping to enter the field must be articulate, have a good memory, and show self-control. It is imperative that they be able to express themselves clearly, remember rapidly changing data that affect their decisions, and be able to operate calmly under very difficult situations involving a great deal of strain. They must also be able to make good, sound, and quickly derived decisions. A poor decision may mean the loss of a large number of lives.

EXPLORING

If you are interested in this career, you can begin exploring by arranging for a visit to an air traffic control center. Many centers welcome and encourage such visits. Talking with air traffic controllers and watching them work will provide you with a strong introduction to their day-to-day activities. Speaking with aircraft pilots may provide other insights into the role of the air traffic controller. Visits and interviews can be arranged through most airports, air traffic control centers, the Air Traffic Control Association, and many airlines. You should also be aware that every branch of the military services offers opportunities for experience in these and related jobs.

EMPLOYERS

Air traffic controllers are employed by the federal government. Most work for the FAA, although a small number work in such areas as the Department of Defense. Approximately 26,000 air traffic controllers work in the United States.

STARTING OUT

The first step in becoming an air traffic controller is taking the written civil service exam, followed by a one-week screening process. Acceptance is on a highly competitive basis. High grades in college or strong work experience are considered essential. Experience in related fields, including those of pilots, air dispatch operators, and other positions with either the civil airlines or the military service will be important for those with—and especially for those without—a college degree. Actual air control experience gained in military service may be a plus. However, civil aviation rules are quite different from military aviation rules. Because the FAA provides complete training, applicants with strong skills and abilities in abstract reasoning, communication, and problem solving, as well as the ability to learn and to work independently, will have the best chance of entering this field.

ADVANCEMENT

After becoming a controller, those who do particularly well may reach the level of supervisor or manager. Many others advance to positions with even more air control responsibilities, and some might move into the top administrative jobs within the FAA. Competitive civil service status can be earned at the end of one year on the job and career status after the satisfactory completion of three years of work in the area.

In the case of both airport control specialists and en route control specialists, the responsibilities become more complex with each successive promotion. Controllers generally begin at the GS-7 level and advance by completing certification requirements for the different air traffic control specialists. New hires at an airport control tower usually begin by communicating flight data and airport conditions to pilots before progressing through the ranks of ground controller, local controller, departure controller, and, lastly, arrival controller. At an en route center, trainees begin by processing flight plans and then advance to become radar associate controllers and, finally, radar controllers.

After becoming fully qualified, controllers who exhibit strong management, organizational, and job skills may advance to become area supervisors and managers and control tower or flight service station managers. Employees in the higher grades may be responsible for a number of different areas, including the coordination of the traffic control activities within the control area, the supervision and training of en route traffic controllers or airport traffic controllers in lower positions, and management in various aeronautical agencies. These positions generally become available after three to five years of fully qualified service.

EARNINGS

Air traffic control trainees start at the GS-7 level, which paid $29,821 annually in 2004. According to the U.S. Department of Labor, in 2002 the average salary for air traffic controllers in nonsupervisory, supervisory, and managerial jobs was $95,700. The lowest paid 10 percent of controllers made less than $46,410. The highest paid controllers made $131,610 or more per year. A controller's experience, job responsibilities, and the complexity of the facility are also factors that influence the rate of pay. Controllers with a great deal of seniority and those at the nation's busiest airports can earn more than $150,000 per year in wages, overtime, and benefits. Controllers may also earn bonuses based on performance.

Because of the complexity of their job duties and the tension involved in their work, air traffic controllers are offered better benefits than other federal employees. Depending on their length of service, air traffic controllers receive 13 to 26 days of paid vacation and 13 days of paid sick leave per year, plus life insurance and health benefits. In addition, they are permitted to retire earlier and with fewer years of service than other federal employees. An air traffic controller with 20 years of experience may retire at the age of 50; those with 25 years of experience may retire at any age. Controllers who manage air traffic are required to retire at age 56. Air traffic controllers who have top skills and experience can receive a retirement exemption up to age 61.

WORK ENVIRONMENT

Air traffic controllers are required to remain constantly alert and focused while performing a large number of simultaneous duties. They must keep track of several aircraft approaching, departing, and passing through the airspace under their control, while receiving flight data from and giving instructions to several pilots at once. They must remain alert to changes in weather and airport conditions, guide planes through intricate approach patterns, and maintain a safe separation of aircraft in the sky and on the ground. They must be able to interpret the symbols on the radar screen, form a clear image of what is happening in the sky above them, and react quickly and decisively to the activity of the aircraft. Controllers must also have strong communicative abilities and be able to give instructions to pilots in a firm and clear tone. The stress of the controller's job requires a great deal of emotional control, especially in times of potential danger and emergency. Traffic conditions change continuously throughout the controller's shift, and the controller must remain alert during times of light traffic as well as times of heavy traffic.

Terminal air traffic controllers work in towers as high as 200 feet off the ground; windows on all sides of the tower allow the controller to see what is happening on the runways and in the sky around the airport. Radar control screens provide locations of all aircraft in the airport's airspace. Large air traffic control towers generally house the radar control center in a room below the observation tower. En route centers are usually housed in large, windowless buildings. These controllers monitor the sky entirely through radar and radio communication. Flight service stations are often located at airports in separate buildings from the control tower.

The numbers of air traffic controllers on duty varies from airport to airport and according to the number of scheduled flights expected in a center's airspace. At a small airport, a controller may work alone for an entire shift; larger airports may have up to 30 controllers on duty, while en route centers may have more than 150 controllers on duty during a shift. Air traffic controllers work a five-day, 40-hour week, usually on a rotating shift basis, which means they often work at night, during the weekends, and during holidays. Overtime is often available; during a shift, controllers are given breaks every two hours.

OUTLOOK

There are two schools of thought regarding the employment outlook for air traffic controllers. The U.S. Department of Labor predicts average growth through 2012 as a result of strong and continued competition for air traffic control positions and the implementation of a new air traffic control system that will reduce employment for workers in the field. On the other hand, the National Air Traffic Controllers Association predicts that employment opportunities will be good over the next seven to eight years as half of the nation's controllers near retirement age. Many industry experts dispute this prediction, arguing that many controllers will stay on after they become eligible for retirement because of good pay and benefits.

Whatever their employment outlook, it is clear that the role of the air traffic controller has begun to change. More and more planes are being equipped with GPS technology. GPS enables pilots to form a far more accurate picture of their position and the position of others in the sky. This allows planes to break away from the traditional air routes and essentially chart their own course, allowing for faster and more economical flights. Under pressure from the airlines, the FAA announced its intentions to adopt a "Free Flight" program, allowing the airlines to take advantage of their GPS equipment. This will mean a far more limited role for the air traffic controller, and especially en route controllers, who may see their functions reduced to monitoring aircraft and stepping in to assist in emergencies. Air traffic controllers will still be needed at the airports, although in fewer numbers. Openings in the field will come primarily from retiring controllers and others who leave the job.

FOR MORE INFORMATION

For information on air traffic control and scholarships, contact
Air Traffic Control Association
1101 King Street, Suite 300
Alexandria, VA 22314
Tel: 703-299-2430
Email: info@atca.org
http://www.atca.org

For career information, contact
Federal Aviation Administration
800 Independence Avenue, SW, Room 810
Washington, DC 20591
Tel: 202-366-4000
http://www.faa.gov/careers

For training information, contact
Federal Aviation Administration Academy
http://www.atctraining.faa.gov

For career and education information, contact
National Air Traffic Controllers Association
1325 Massachusetts Avenue, NW
Washington, DC 20005
Tel: 202-628-545
http://www.natca.org

For information on air traffic control and industry publications, contact
National Association of Air Traffic Specialists
11303 Amherst Avenue, Suite 4
Wheaton, MD 20902
Tel: 301-933-6228
http://www.naats.org

For information on air traffic control careers in Canada, contact the following associations:
Canadian Air Traffic Control Association
162 Cleopatra Drive
Nepean, ON K2G 5X2 Canada
Tel: 613-225-3553
Email: catca@catca.ca
http://www.catca.ca

Nav Canada
PO Box 3411, Station D
Ottawa, ON K1P 5L6 Canada
Tel: 800-876-4693
http://www.navcanada.ca

=========================== **INTERVIEW** ===========================

Tom Coronite has been an air traffic controller for 13 years. He spoke with the editors of Careers in Focus: Aviation *about his career.*

Q. Please briefly describe your primary and secondary job duties.

A. I work in a tower cab, so my primary duties involve the sequencing and separation of aircraft on the ground, that is, on runways and taxiways, and in our "Class B" airspace, which is from 0 to 2,000 feet in an eight-mile radius centered on the airport. I accomplish this by working local control, in which I clear planes for landings and takeoffs, and ground control, in which I taxi planes to their gates or to their takeoff runways, issuing routes so all the planes keep moving efficiently and the airport doesn't get clogged up. We also have clearance delivery and flight data, which handle flight plans clearances and disseminate various bits of information.

My secondary duties would include the various training items I must keep current on, as well as some administrative tasks I am assigned from time to time, like special workgroups and specific projects. Since I am also the union's facility representative, I am also afforded some time each week to perform representational duties, such as handling employee grievances and various meetings with the facility manager.

Q. What was your educational path?

A. Mine was different than most; I was not planning a career in aviation. I went to Boston College to study chemistry, but left college after a year. I later entered the seminary to become a Roman Catholic priest. There I received a B.S. in philosophy, and then a master of divinity (theology) degree. Many controllers have some college education, many do not. The minimum educational requirement is a high school diploma. Some controllers do go to college and study in aviation fields before an ATC career, but it certainly isn't necessary.

Q. How did you train for this job?

A. First, I had to take a civil service exam and get a high enough score to be hired. Then, when I was hired by the Federal Aviation Administration (FAA), I was sent to the FAA Academy in Oklahoma City, Oklahoma, for a nine-week screening process. This was designed to evaluate whether or not I had the skills to be successful at air traffic control (ATC). Once I successfully completed that screening, I received some basic training for the type of facility I was going to—in my case a tower. When I arrived at my first facility, there was some classroom training, followed by on-the-job training (OJT), in which I talked to the airplanes' crew with a veteran controller backing me up. In my first facility, it took me about seven months to complete training. When I went to my next facility, the process of classroom and OJT training started all over, and it took me about a year to complete training. Occasionally it does happen that a controller is unsuccessful in his training, and returns to his previous facility.

Q. Where did you get your first job in this field? What did you do?

A. After I completed the nine-week screening in Oklahoma, I was assigned as a controller at New Haven, Connecticut. There is a very small airport there that mostly handles general aviation traffic and a lot of student pilots. As I mentioned before, I had some classroom training, then I "plugged in" with one of the veterans training me. In training, I performed all the duties of an ATC in the tower cab: flight data, clearance delivery, and ground and local control. Occasionally a controller in charge also has to perform the supervisory functions when no supervisors are available or on duty. That was the case at New Haven and also at my current facility at Logan Airport (Boston, Massachusetts).

Q. What kind of resources are available to people who are interested in learning more about becoming an air traffic controller?

A. The website of the National Air Traffic Controllers Association (http://www.natca.net), our union, is a great source of information. The FAA's site (http:/www.faa.gov) may also be helpful.

Q. What qualities do air traffic controllers need to be successful in the field?

A. In my humble opinion, the most important quality for this job is being able to think on your feet. Very often what we do is regimented and orderly, to the point of being routine. However, when something goes wrong, or something out of the ordinary happens, you need to act fast and keep the planes separated. That's job #1! You often don't have time to ask for advice or even weigh options. You must pick the best option immediately, take charge, and do it. You must be able to make snap decisions. You must be able to project the consequences of your decisions and plan ahead, but also be able to quickly come up with a "plan B" if what you originally planned isn't working. You need to be able to listen, talk, write, think, all at the same time, and do them quickly.

On the personal side, you need to be a team player. ATC is not an individual sport: It's a team game. Your actions affect the controller next to you, and vice versa. Next rotation, you may be in his spot and he in yours. You need to know what the guy next to you has going on and anticipate his needs. A good air traffic controller is a good teammate. You also need to have a thick skin! Things sometimes get hectic and boisterous. You need to be on your toes, and be prepared to be criticized when you're not. But everyone is in that spot at one time or another, so you need to take your lumps and move on.

Q. What are some of the pros and cons of your job?

A. Air traffic control is an exciting and rewarding career. It's mentally challenging, and you can go home at the end of the day with a sense of satisfaction that you made a difference. And you can leave your work at work—no projects sitting on a desk waiting to be finished. Depending on where you work, the salary can be quite good (more than $100,000 a year), but you sure do earn it! On the con side, you'll likely do shift work, and that can be draining. It can also negatively impact family life. You'll likely work weekends, holidays, and graveyard shifts. At times it can be very stressful, and you need to find healthy ways of dealing with the stress. Chances are, you won't find many in your neighborhood who are familiar with the profession and can commiserate with you.

Q. What is the most important piece of advice that you have to offer young people who are interested in this field?

A. Be patient. It can sometimes take a long time to get to the facility you really want. And be flexible. I can't imagine anything more stressful than doing a job you're not suited for. If ATC isn't for you, it isn't. It's not for everyone. Be able to admit that if it really is the case. But if you are suited for it, hang in there until you get where you want to be. I'm where I always wanted to be, and I love it.

Q. What is the future employment outlook for air traffic controllers?

A. This is a tough one to answer. On the horizon is a potential shortage, as many controllers who were hired after the '81 strike become eligible for retirement. The FAA seems to be ignoring this potential shortage. Will they see it, wake up, and hire more controllers? That's anybody's guess. But with air traffic projected to be on the rise, it's likely that more controllers will be needed. President Bush has made some definite movements toward trying to privatize the ATC system. The National Air Traffic Controllers Association believes this would be an unwise move as it could put safety in a position of being secondary to profit and the bottom line. We fully support keeping controllers as government employees, who will always be able to proudly proclaim SAFETY as job #1!

As long as that continues to be the case, there should always be a spot for another controller, ready to do all it takes to keep the skies safe.

Aviation Safety Inspectors

OVERVIEW

The regulations of the Federal Aviation Administration are enforced by *aviation safety inspectors* who usually specialize in general aviation or commercial aircraft. They inspect maintenance, manufacturing, repair, and operations procedures and also certify pilots, flight instructors, flight examiners, repair facilities, and aviation schools. They are responsible for the quality and safety of aircraft equipment and personnel. Aviation safety inspectors are classified under the heading of *transportation inspectors*. There are approximately 29,000 transportation inspectors in the United States.

HISTORY

Although the U.S. Constitution gives Congress the power to regulate and control interstate travel via the highway, railway, and water, it does not mention anything about the air. Indeed, the framers of that document did not foresee the age of air travel that would begin in a little more than 100 years. The Wright brothers may have flown the first airplane in 1903, but air travel was not regulated until 1926 when the Secretary of Commerce was given the authority to create a regulatory system. This system was the precursor to the agencies that would later employ many aviation safety inspectors. The system evolved as much as it could to keep pace with the burgeoning field of air transportation until the 1950s, when it could no longer handle the rapidly occurring changes in the field and became outdated. To address these changes, the Federal Aviation Agency was created in 1958. The Federal Aviation Agency was given the authority to promote the development and safety of air transportation through regulations. One of its responsibilities is to set and enforce safety standards. It later became a part of the Department of Transportation (DOT) and was renamed the Federal Aviation Administration (FAA). Another government agency concerned with aviation safety, the National Transportation Safety Board (NTSB), was established in 1967 as a part of the DOT and was made an independent agency in 1975. The NTSB is responsible for investigating aviation accidents, determining the probable cause of accidents, and making recommendations for safety improvements in the field of aviation. Outside of the United States, the growing need for air safety issues and regulations was addressed by the creation of the International Civil Aviation Organization (ICAO) in 1947, and the International Air Transport Association (IATA) in 1945.

THE JOB

The duties of an aviation safety inspector generally include making sure that aircraft are airworthy, that the facilities and equipment surrounding aircraft are safe, and that the personnel working on or flying aircraft complete their work safely and correctly. The specific duties of aviation safety inspectors depend on the area in which they specialize.

Aviation safety inspectors usually work in one of three general areas: operations, pertaining to the operation of aircraft; manufacturing, pertaining to the manufacture of aircraft or related equipment; or airworthiness, pertaining to the maintenance and repair of aircraft and related equipment in order to ensure safe flight. In addition, the FAA has identified and defined eight different types of aviation safety inspectors: *general aviation avionics inspectors, general aviation maintenance inspectors, general aviation operations inspectors, air carrier avionics inspectors, air carrier maintenance inspectors, air carrier operations inspectors, manufacturing inspectors,* and *cabin safety inspectors.* These inspectors all administer and enforce safety regulations and uphold set standards. The differences are in the general areas that the inspectors regulate and/or the size of the aircraft they inspect.

Aviation safety inspectors working in operations are concerned with the people operating aircraft and their training programs, equipment, and facilities. The inspector evaluates pilots, navigators, and flight instructors and issues initial certification that they are proficient and meet the necessary requirements. This certification is done on a continuing basis, and the inspector is responsible for that as well. They also evaluate the manner in which these workers are trained, the equipment they use, and the facilities in which they work and train to make sure they meet safety regulations and standards. One way an inspector might do this is by running simulations with flight personnel, ground crews, and air traffic controllers to monitor performance of the people and equipment involved.

Aviation safety inspectors working in manufacturing are concerned with the design and manufacture of aircraft, aircraft parts, and avionics equipment. They examine these materials to make sure they match the necessary design specifications. Inspectors may use hand tools and test instruments to accomplish this. They also issue the original certificates determining airworthiness for all aircraft. Inspectors in this area also inspect manufacturing facilities to make sure they meet safety regulations and standards.

Aviation safety inspectors working in airworthiness are concerned with the repair and maintenance of aircraft, aircraft parts, and avionics equipment. They assess the skills of the mechanics that work on aircraft and related parts and equipment and issue initial certification that they are proficient and meet the necessary requirements. This certification is done on a continuing basis, and the inspector is responsible for that as well. They are also responsible for assessing and certifying repair facilities and evaluating mechanic training programs. Inspectors perform inspections of aircraft to determine airworthiness, checking for any problems due to damage or deficient components. One way they do this is by starting the aircraft being inspected and observing the gauges, meters, and other instruments to ensure they are working properly. These inspectors are also responsible for examining maintenance programs and facilities, the equipment and procedures used for maintenance, and maintenance schedules. They advise whether new equipment needs to be acquired or if existing equipment needs to be fixed or modified. They check maintenance records and flight logs to see if prescribed service and maintenance procedures were performed and completed in a timely manner.

REQUIREMENTS

High School

High school students interested in a career in aviation safety should pursue a college prep curriculum, since a college degree is preferred for many positions in aviation safety inspection. Mathematics and science courses are especially useful. Coursework in communications will also be beneficial, since aviation safety inspectors need to ask questions, instruct others, and give oral and written reports of their findings.

Postsecondary Training

A high school diploma or equivalent is the minimum eligibility requirement for all federal aviation safety positions; a college degree may be required for nongovernment positions. Experience is also required, some of which is general to all aviation safety positions. Other experience is specific to the different positions in the field of aviation safety. A college education can be used to substitute for some or all of the required experience, depending upon each position. For example, the federal government will allow the substitution of one year of school for nine months of general experience. A bachelor's degree in the fields of engineering, aeronautics, or air transportation is especially useful. All prospective aviation safety inspectors should have general experience that provides them with knowledge of the aviation industry and/or aircraft operation. Examples of positions that would qualify as general experience include being a pilot or crew member, an air traffic controller, an aviation mechanic, or an avionics technician.

Some positions require specific experience. For example, an aviation safety inspector in operations needs experience as a pilot or copilot, a flight instructor, a flight test pilot, a flight inspector, or an aviation operations inspector. Some positions require that inspectors have the ability to operate specific types of aircraft. This experience can be gained from private flight schools, university flight schools, and military training.

An aviation safety inspector in manufacturing needs experience with quality control in accordance with federal aviation regulations. The quality control experience should be with the production of aircraft, aircraft engines, aircraft propellers, or aircraft assemblies. Some positions require additional experience in supervision, management, and implementation of quality control programs.

An aviation safety inspector focusing on airworthiness needs experience in supervising the repair and maintenance of aircraft, aircraft engines, or aircraft electronics communications and navigation systems. This experience must include being responsible for following federal aviation standards for airworthiness, or military regulations and safety standards. A job as a field service representative of an aircraft systems manufacturer or an aircraft equipment manufacturer may provide adequate experience for some positions, as well.

Certification and Licensing

Certification requirements vary according to the position. For example, an aviation safety inspector working for the federal government in a position where he or she has to operate aircraft must have a commercial pilot certificate as well as a flight instructor certificate, both with single and multi-engine land and instrument ratings. An aviation safety inspector in a position where he or she has to operate aircraft in the air carrier field must have an airline transport pilot certificate. A commercial pilot certificate with multi-engine land and instrument ratings, and eligibility for an airline transport pilot certificate will also suffice. Aviation safety inspectors in the area of manufacturing, working for the federal government at a GS-9 position or above, need an FAA mechanic certificate, with airframe and powerplant ratings. All certificates must be current.

Other Requirements

Aviation safety inspectors must be methodical, have an eye for detail, and be able to accept responsibility. They must be persistent and patient as they perform inspections or follow an investigation to its conclusion. They also must be able to communicate well with others in order to reach a clear analysis of a situation and be able to report this information. Inspectors must be able to write effective reports that convey vast amounts of information and investigative work.

For many careers in aviation safety, United States citizenship is required, as well as the ability to pass a background security check. Some positions have a minimum age requirement.

EXPLORING

If you are interested in this career, you can begin exploring by arranging to shadow an aviation safety inspector at work. Talking with aviation safety inspectors and observing them as they work will give you a sampling of their duties, as well as the type of situations they encounter from day to day. Visits and interviews can be arranged through the FAA. Another option that will help you learn about aviation safety inspectors is to arrange to take a tour of an airport. Many aviation safety inspectors began with jobs such as aircraft pilots, air traffic controllers, and aviation mechanics or repair workers. Visiting an airport and taking a tour will give you a broader understanding of the basis of aviation safety and will enable you to observe how aviation safety issues affect those careers and the public travelers who pass in and out of an airport on a daily basis.

Visits can be arranged through most airports and many airlines, although there might be limitations due to security concerns. You should be aware that every branch of the military services offers opportunities for vital experience for these jobs, and many jobs that are closely related.

EMPLOYERS

Most aviation safety inspectors are employed by the federal government, with the majority working for the Department of Transportation, namely the FAA, and the NTSB. Other employers of aviation safety inspectors include consulting firms, insurance companies, and companies that specialize in aviation technology and industry. Some inspectors are self-employed and work as independent consultants. Aviation safety inspectors are classified under the heading of transportation inspectors. There are approximately 29,000 transportation inspectors in the United States.

STARTING OUT

Aviation safety inspectors are generally not hired unless they have experience in the field of aviation, for example, as a pilot or crew member, an air traffic controller, an aviation mechanic, an avionics technician, or a manufacturing position in the aviation industry. A combination of work experience in the field of aviation and education in areas such as air transportation, engineering, or aeronautics will count as sufficient experience in some cases. After gaining the necessary experience, those interested in becoming an aviation safety inspector should apply for a position. One of the largest employers of aviation safety inspectors, the FAA, maintains a national register of qualified applicants. Persons interested in being hired by the FAA as an aviation safety inspector should contact the FAA for an application. Applicants who are deemed qualified and eligible for employment are placed on the national register for a period of one year. They are matched to any available job vacancies that fit their qualifications.

ADVANCEMENT

Aviation safety inspectors who demonstrate superior job skills may be promoted to positions with an increase in salary and greater responsibility. Those who exhibit managerial skills may advance to a supervisory position, such as section or branch chief. Inspectors with strong teaching and training skills may become instructors at the FAA Academy. Aviation safety inspectors who have a recognized level of expertise may opt to work for themselves as independent consultants.

EARNINGS

Transportation inspectors had median annual earnings of $48,500 in 2002, according to the U.S. Department of Labor. Salaries ranged from less than $21,900 to $55,800 or more annually.

Aviation safety inspectors receive typical fringe benefits, which may include medical and dental insurance, life insurance, sick days, paid vacation days, and participation in a 401(k) or similar savings plan. In addition, government employees may receive a pension. Self-employed aviation safety inspectors are responsible for their own insurance and savings needs.

WORK ENVIRONMENT

The work environment of an aviation safety inspector varies, depending on their employment situation. They usually work both indoors and outdoors, depending on the location and subject of the inspection or investigation. Many aviation safety inspectors who work for the government, consulting firms, or who are self-employed spend much time in the field and therefore will travel a great deal. Since they are responsible for inspecting aircraft and aircraft facilities, they will need to travel to the necessary locations in order to perform an inspection. Aviation safety inspectors investigating an accident will need to travel to the accident site. Aviation safety inspectors working for private companies may not need to travel as much, since many of their job duties will be performed in-house. Aviation safety inspectors need to be able to work independently and as part of a team, since both qualities are warranted in different job situations. A normal workweek for an aviation safety inspector is 40 hours. However, additional hours may be necessary, for example, to finish an important inspection or to investigate an accident.

OUTLOOK

The U.S. Department of Labor predicts slower-than-average growth for all transportation inspectors. Employment opportunities should be slightly better for aviation safety inspectors as the federal government seeks to improve aviation safety and address security threats.

FOR MORE INFORMATION

For career information, contact
Federal Aviation Administration
800 Independence Avenue, SW, Room 810
Washington, DC 20591
Tel: 202-366-4000
http://www.faa.gov/careers

INTERVIEW

Mike McKenna recently attended the Institute of Aviation, University of Illinois-Urbana Champaign. He talked with the editors of Careers in Focus: Aviation *about his educational experiences.*

Q. What made you want to study aviation?

A. When I was in high school, I knew that I either wanted to be an engineer or to fly. When the chance to fly in college became a reality at the University of Illinois, I thought that it was a great opportunity to study a unique field.

Q. Please describe your classroom and flight studies.

A. We had ground school twice a week for approximately two hours per session. The instructor discussed various topics pertaining to the current flight class in which students were enrolled. We flew three times a week for two hours each session. We also flew on the weekends.

Q. Did you participate in any internships?

A. I was very fortunate to participate in an internship with the National Transportation Safety Board. My duties included assisting investigators throughout the process of determining causes for accidents.

Q. What advice would you give students who are interested in aviation?

A. My best advice is do not major solely in an aviation-related field. For example, if you are interested in aviation management, I think it is best to get a basic business degree in addition to your various pilot licenses. Also, many students also major in engineering while pursuing a pilot license. These students are the most marketable after graduation.

Q. What are your future employment plans?

A. I plan to enter the field of aviation safety investigation. My internship made me very interested in this field.

Avionics Engineers and Technicians

QUICK FACTS

School Subjects
Mathematics
Technical/shop

Personal Skills
Mechanical/manipulative
Technical/scientific

Work Environment
Primarily indoors
Primarily one location

Minimum Education Level
Bachelor's degree (engineers)
Some postsecondary training
(technicians)

Salary Range
$49,640 to $72,750 to
$105,060+ (engineers)
$29,130 to $42,030 to
$56,150+ (technicians)

Certification or Licensing
Required by all states
(engineers)
Required for certain
positions (technicians)

Outlook
Decline (engineers)
More slowly than the average
(technicians)

DOT
823

(continues)

OVERVIEW

Avionics (from the words *aviation* and *electronics*) is the application of electronics to the operation of aircraft, spacecraft, and missiles. *Avionics engineers* conduct research and solve developmental problems associated with aviation, such as instrument landing systems and other safety instruments. Avionics engineers are subspecialty of the field of aerospace engineering. There are approximately 78,000 aerospace engineers in the United States.

Avionics technicians inspect, test, adjust, and repair the electronic components of aircraft communications, navigation, and flight-control systems and compile complete maintenance-and-overhaul records for the work they do. Avionics technicians also calibrate and adjust the frequencies of communications apparatus when it is installed and perform periodic checks on those frequency settings. Avionics technicians hold about 25,600 jobs.

HISTORY

The field of avionics began in World War II, when military aircraft were operated for the first time using electronic equipment. Rockets were also being developed during this time, and these devices required electronic systems to control their flight. As aircraft rapidly grew more complicated, the amount of electronic apparatus needed for navigation and for monitoring equipment performance greatly increased. The World War II B-29 bomber carried 2,000 to

3,000 avionic components; the B-52 of the Vietnam era carried 50,000; later, the B-58 supersonic bomber required more than 95,000. As the military grew increasingly reliant on electronic systems, specialists were required to build, install, operate, and repair them.

The development of large ballistic missiles during and after World War II and the rapid growth of the U.S. space program after 1958 increased development of avionics technology. Large missiles and spacecraft require many more electronic components than even the largest and most sophisticated aircraft. Computerized guidance systems became especially important with the advent of manned spaceflights. Avionics technology was also applied to civil aircraft. The race to be the first in space and, later, to be the first to land on the moon stimulated the need for trained specialists to work with newer and more complex electronic technology. The push for achieving military superiority during the Cold War era also created a demand for avionics specialists and technicians. The commercial airline industry has been growing rapidly since the 1950s; since that time, more and more planes have been built, and the drive to provide greater comfort and safety for passengers has created an even greater demand for avionics engineers and technicians.

Avionics continues to be an important branch of aeronautical and astronautical engineering. The aerospace industry places great emphasis on research and development, assigning a much higher percentage of its trained technical personnel to this effort than is usual in industry. In addition, stringent safety regulations require constant surveillance of in-service equipment. For these reasons there is a high demand for trained and experienced avionics engineers and technicians to help in the development of new satellites, spacecraft, aircraft, and their component electronic systems and to maintain those in service.

QUICK FACTS

(continued)

GOE
05.05.10

NOC
2244

O*NET-SOC
17-2011.00, 17-3021.00, 49-2091.00

THE JOB

Avionics engineers develop new electronic systems and components for aerospace use. Avionics technicians assist engineers in these developments. They also adapt existing systems and components for application in new equipment. For the most part, however, they install, test, repair, and maintain navigation, communications, and control apparatus in existing aircraft and spacecraft.

Technicians use apparatus such as circuit analyzers and oscilloscopes to test and replace such sophisticated equipment as transceivers and Doppler radar systems, as well as microphones, headsets, and other standard electronic communications apparatus. New equipment, once installed, must be tested and calibrated to prescribed specifications. Technicians also adjust the frequencies of radio sets and other communications equipment by signaling ground stations and then adjusting set screws until the desired frequency has been achieved. Periodic maintenance checks and readjustments enable avionics technicians to keep equipment operating on proper frequencies. The technicians also complete and sign maintenance-and-overhaul documents recording the history of various equipment.

Avionics engineers and technicians involved in the design and testing of a new apparatus must take into account all operating conditions, determining weight limitations, resistance to physical shock, the atmospheric conditions the device will have to withstand, and other factors. For some sophisticated projects, technicians will have to design and make their tools first and then use them to construct and test new avionic components.

The range of equipment in the avionics field is so broad that technicians usually specialize in one area, such as radio equipment, radar, computerized guidance, or flight-control systems. New specialty areas are constantly opening up as innovations occur in avionics. The development of these new specialty areas requires technicians to keep informed by reading technical articles and books and by attending seminars and courses about the new developments, which are often sponsored by manufacturers.

Avionics technicians usually work as part of a team, especially if involved in research, testing, and development of new products. They are often required to keep notes and records of their work and to write detailed reports.

REQUIREMENTS

High School
Persons interested in pursuing a career in avionics should take high school mathematics courses at least through solid geometry and preferably through calculus. They should take English, speech, and communications classes in order to read complex and detailed technical articles, books, and reports; to write technical reports; and to present those reports to groups of people when required. Many schools offer shop classes in electronics and in diagram and blueprint reading.

Postsecondary Training

Avionics engineers must have a bachelor's degree from an accredited college or university and may participate in a cooperative education program through their engineering school. Avionics technicians must have completed a course of training at a postsecondary technical institute or community college. The training should include at least one year of electronics technician training. If not trained specifically in avionics, students should obtain a solid background in electronics theory and practice. Further specialized training will be done on the job, where technicians work with engineers and senior technicians until they are competent to work without direct supervision.

Larger corporations in the aerospace industry operate their own schools and training institutes. Such training rarely includes theoretical or general studies but concentrates on areas important to the company's functions. The U.S. armed forces also conduct excellent electronics and avionics training schools; their graduates are in high demand in the industry after they leave the service.

Certification or Licensing

All states require engineers to be licensed. There are two levels of licensing for engineers. Professional engineers (PEs) have graduated from an accredited engineering curriculum, have four years of engineering experience, and have passed a written exam. Engineering graduates need not wait until they have four years experience, however, to start the licensure process. Those who pass the Fundamentals of Engineering examination after graduating are called engineers in training (EITs) or engineer interns or intern engineers. The EIT certification usually is valid for 10 years. After acquiring suitable work experience, EITs can take the second examination, the Principles and Practice of Engineering exam, to gain full PE licensure.

In order to ensure that avionics engineers are kept up to date on their quickly changing field, many states have imposed continuing education requirements for relicensure.

Federal Communications Commission (FCC) regulations require that anyone who works with radio transmitting equipment have a restricted radiotelephone operator's license. Such a license is issued upon application to the FCC and is issued for life.

Other Requirements

To be successful in this work, you should have strong science and mathematics skills. In addition, you will need to have good manual dexterity and mechanical aptitude and the temperament for exacting work.

An avionics technician calibrates the settings on a communications system in a small plane. *(Mathew Hohmann)*

EXPLORING

One good way to learn more about avionics is to visit factories and test facilities where avionics technicians work as part of teams designing and testing new equipment. It is also possible to visit a large airfield's repair facilities where avionics technicians inspect, maintain, and calibrate communications and control apparatus. You can also arrange to visit other types of electronics manufacturers.

Useful information about avionics training programs and career opportunities is available from the U.S. armed forces as well as from trade and technical schools and community colleges that offer such programs. These organizations are always pleased to answer inquiries from prospective students or service personnel.

EMPLOYERS

About half of the 78,000 aerospace engineers employed in the United States work in the aerospace product and parts manufacturing industries. About 10 percent are employed in federal government agencies, primarily the Department of Defense and the National Aeronautics and Space Administration. Other employers include engineering and architectural services, research and testing services, and search and navigation equipment firms.

There are approximately 25,600 avionics technicians employed in the United States. Most technicians work for airlines or airports and flying fields. Other major employers include the federal government and aircraft assembly firms.

STARTING OUT

Those entering the field of avionics must first obtain the necessary training in electronics. Following that training, the school's career services department can help locate prospective employers, arrange interviews, and advise about an employment search. Other possibilities are to contact an employment agency or to approach a prospective employer directly. Service in the military is an excellent way to gain education, training, and experience in avionics; many companies are eager to hire technicians with a military background.

ADVANCEMENT

Avionics technicians usually begin their careers in trainee positions until they are thoroughly familiar with the requirements and routines of their work. Having completed their apprenticeships, they are usually assigned to work independently, with only minimal supervision, doing testing and repair work. The most experienced and able technicians go on to install new equipment and to work in research and development operations. Many senior technicians move into training, supervisory, sales, and customer relations positions. Some choose to pursue additional training and become avionics engineers.

Avionics engineers are already at an advanced position but may move up to become engineering supervisors or managers.

EARNINGS

The U.S. Department of Labor reports that median annual earnings of aerospace engineers (the category under which the department classifies avionics engineers) were $72,750 in 2002. Salaries ranged from less than $49,640 to more than $105,060. Median annual earnings of engineers who worked for the federal government were $81,830. Engineers who worked in the aerospace product and parts manufacturing industry earned $70,920.

Median earnings of avionics technicians were $42,030 in 2002, according to the U.S. Department of Labor. The top 10 percent of technicians earned more than $56,150 a year. The lowest 10 percent earned less than $29,130 a year. Federal government employees (not including armed forces personnel) on the average earn slightly less than avionics technicians employed by private aerospace firms. Their jobs, however, are more secure.

WORK ENVIRONMENT

Avionics engineers and technicians work for aircraft and aerospace manufacturers, airlines, and NASA and other government agencies. Most avionics engineers and technicians specialize in a specific area of avionics; they are also responsible for keeping up with the latest technological and industry advances. Their work is usually performed in pleasant indoor surroundings. Because this work is very precise, successful engineers and technicians must have a personality suited to meeting exact standards. Technicians sometimes work in closely cooperating teams. This requires an ability to work with a team spirit of coordinated effort.

OUTLOOK

The U.S. Department of Labor predicts that employment for avionics engineers will decline through 2012. Slower-than-average employment growth is expected for avionics technicians during this same time period.

The aerospace industry is closely tied to government spending and to political change, as well as to the economy, which also affects the aircraft and airline industries strongly. The decline in airline travel in recent years has led to reduced employment opportunities for avionics engineers and technicians.

Despite this decline, avionics is an important and constantly developing field for which more and more trained engineers and technicians will be required. Reliance on electronic technology has grown rapidly and in virtually every industry. Many defense contractors have begun to branch out into other products, especially in the areas of electronic and computer technology. Commercial applications of the space program, including the launching of privately owned satellites, are also providing new opportunities in the aerospace industry.

FOR MORE INFORMATION

For a list of accredited schools and colleges, contact
Accreditation Board for Engineering and Technology Inc.
111 Market Place, Suite 1050
Baltimore, MD 21202-4102
Tel: 410-347-7700
http://www.abet.org

For information about scholarships, colleges, and career opportunities, contact the following:

Aerospace Education Foundation
1501 Lee Highway
Arlington, VA 22209-1198
Tel: 703-247-5839
Email: aefstaff@aef.org
http://www.aef.org

Contact AIA for publications with information on aerospace technologies, careers, and space.

Aerospace Industries Association
    of America
1000 Wilson Boulevard, Suite 1700
Arlington, VA 22209-3901
Tel: 703-358-1000
http://www.aia-aerospace.org

For career information and details on student branches of this organization, contact

American Institute of Aeronautics
    and Astronautics
1801 Alexander Bell Drive, Suite 500
Reston, VA 20191-4344
Tel: 800-639-2422
http://www.aiaa.org

For information on educational programs and to purchase a copy of Engineering: Go For It, *contact*

American Society for Engineering Education
1818 N Street, NW
Washington, DC 20036
Tel: 202-331-3500
http://www.asee.org

For information on general aviation, contact

General Aviation Manufacturers
    Association
1400 K Street, NW, Suite 801
Washington, DC 20005
Tel: 202-393-1500
http://www.generalaviation.org

For information on careers and student competitions, contact
Junior Engineering Technical Society
1420 King Street, Suite 405
Alexandria, VA 22314
Tel: 703-548-5387
Email: info@jets.org
http://www.jets.org

For career and licensing information, contact
National Society of Professional Engineers
1420 King Street
Alexandria, VA 22314-2794
Tel: 703-684-2800
http://www.nspe.org/students

For career information, see AIAC's website.
Aerospace Industries Association of Canada (AIAC)
60 Queen Street, #1200
Ottawa, ON K1P 5Y7 Canada
Email: info@aiac.ca
http://www.aiac.ca

Customs Officials

OVERVIEW

Customs officials are federal workers who are employed by the United States Bureau of Customs and Border Protection (a branch of the Department of Homeland Security) to prevent terrorists and terrorist weapons from entering the United States, enforce laws governing imports and exports, and to combat smuggling and revenue fraud. Amid a whirl of international travel and commercial activity, customs officials process travelers, baggage, cargo, and mail, as well as administer certain navigation laws. Stationed in the United States and overseas at airports, seaports, and all crossings, as well as at points along the Canadian and Mexican borders, customs officials examine, count, weigh, gauge, measure, and sample commercial and noncommercial cargoes entering and leaving the United States. It is their job to determine whether or not goods are admissible and, if so, how much tax, or duty, should be assessed on them. To prevent terrorism, smuggling, fraud, and cargo theft, customs officials also check the individual baggage declarations of international travelers and oversee the unloading of all types of commercial shipments. More than 40,000 customs workers are employed by Customs and Border Protection.

QUICK FACTS

School Subjects
English
Foreign language
Government

Personal Skills
Helping/teaching
Leadership/management

Work Environment
Indoors and outdoors
Primarily multiple locations

Minimum Education Level
Some postsecondary training

Salary Range
$24,075 to $44,136 to $52,899+

Certification or Licensing
None available

Outlook
Faster than the average

DOT
168

GOE
04.01.02

NOC
1236

O*NET-SOC
33-3021.05

HISTORY

Countries collect taxes on imports and sometimes on exports as a means of producing revenue for the government. Export duties were first introduced in England in the year 1275 by a statute that levied taxes on animal hides and on wool. American colonists in the 1700s objected to the import duties England forced them to pay (levied under the Townshend Acts), charging "taxation without representation." Although the British government rescinded the Townshend Acts, it retained the tax on tea, which led to the Boston Tea Party on December 16, 1773.

After the American Revolution, delegates at the Constitutional Convention decided that "no tax or duty shall be laid on articles exported from any state," but they approved taxing imports from abroad. The customs service was established by the First Congress in 1789 as part of the Treasury Department. Until 1816 these customs assessments were used primarily for revenue. The Tariff Act of 1816 declared, however, that the main function of customs laws was to protect American industry from foreign companies. By 1927 the customs service was established as a separate bureau within the Treasury Department.

Following the terrorist attacks of September 11, 2001, national attention was drawn to the need for heightened and new security at

On a Typical Day, the U.S. Customs and Border Protection Service . . .

Processes:
- more than 1.1 million passengers
- more than 57,006 trucks/containers
- 580 vessels
- 2,459 aircraft
- 323,622 vehicles

Executes more than:
- 64 arrests
- 118 narcotics seizures
- 11 currency seizures
- 116 other seizures (conveyances, ammunition, commercial merchandise, real estate, firearms and weapons, and child pornography)

Seizes:
- 4,639 pounds of narcotics
- more than $23,083 in arms and ammunition
- $467,118 in merchandise
- $715,652 in currency

Source: U.S. Bureau of Customs and Border Protection, 2002

U.S. borders, in U.S. airports, and in dealing with travelers throughout the United States. Many governmental agencies, including the U.S. Customs Service, were restructured to better face this new threat. In 2003, the U.S. Customs Service was merged with portions of the Department of Agriculture, the Immigration and Naturalization Service, and the Border Patrol and renamed the Bureau of Customs and Border Protection (CBP). CBP became an official bureau of the Department of Homeland Security on March 1, 2003. According to its website, CBP's new primary responsibility, in addition to controlling imports and exports, is to prevent international terrorist groups from securing weapons of mass destruction, arms and munitions, funds, and other support that could be used to commit acts of terrorism.

THE JOB

Customs officials perform a wide variety of duties including preventing terrorists and terrorist weapons from entering the United States, controlling imports and exports, and combating smuggling and revenue fraud.

As a result of its merger in 2003 with several other protective and monitoring agencies of the U.S. government, the bureau of Customs and Border Protection has created a new position, the *customs and border protection (CBP) officer,* which consolidates the skills and responsibilities of three positions in these agencies: the customs inspector, the immigration officer, and the agricultural inspector. These workers are uniformed and armed. A second new position, the *CBP agriculture specialist* has been created to complement the work of the CBP officer. CBP Agriculture Specialists are uniformed, but not armed.

CBP officers conduct surveillance at points of entry into the United States to prohibit smuggling, detect customs violations, and deter acts of terrorism. They try to catch people illegally transporting smuggled merchandise and contraband such as narcotics, watches, jewelry, chemicals, and weapons, as well as fruits, plants, and meat that may be infested with pests or diseases. On the waterfront, officers monitor piers, ships, and crew members and are constantly on the lookout for items being thrown from the ship to small boats nearby. Customs patrol officers provide security at entrance and exit facilities of piers and airports, make sure all baggage is checked, and maintain security at loading, exit, and entrance areas of customs buildings and during the transfer of legal drug shipments to prevent hijackings or theft. Using informers and other sources, they gather intelligence information about illegal activities. When probable cause exists, they are authorized to take possible violators into custody, using physical force or weapons if necessary. They assist other customs personnel in developing or testing new enforcement techniques and equipment.

CBP officers also are responsible for carefully and thoroughly examining cargo to make sure that it matches the description on a ship's or aircraft's manifest. They inspect baggage and personal items worn or carried by travelers entering or leaving the United States by ship, plane, or automobile. CBP officers are authorized to go aboard a ship or plane to determine the exact nature of the cargo being transported. In the course of a single day they review cargo manifests, inspect cargo containers, and supervise unloading activities to prevent terrorism, smuggling, fraud, or cargo thefts. They may have to weigh and measure imports to see that commerce laws are being followed and to protect American distributors in cases where restricted trademarked merchandise is being brought into the country. In this way, they can protect the interests of American companies.

CBP officers examine crew and passenger lists, sometimes in cooperation with the police or security personnel from federal government agencies, who may be searching for criminals or terrorists. They are authorized to search suspicious individuals and to arrest these offenders if necessary. They are also allowed to conduct body searches of suspected individuals to check for contraband. They check health clearances and ships' documents in an effort to prevent the spread of disease that may require quarantine.

Individual baggage declarations of international travelers also come under their scrutiny. CBP officers who have baggage examination duty at points of entry into the United States classify purchases made abroad and, if necessary, assess and collect duties. All international travelers are allowed to bring home certain quantities of foreign purchases, such as perfume, clothing, tobacco, and liquor, without paying taxes. However, they must declare the amount and value of their purchases on a customs form. If they have made purchases above the duty-free limits, they must pay taxes. CBP officers are prepared to advise tourists about U.S. customs regulations and allow them to change their customs declarations if necessary and pay the duty before baggage inspection. CBP officers must be alert and observant to detect undeclared items. If any are discovered, it is up to the officer to decide whether an oversight or deliberate fraud has occurred. Sometimes the contraband is held and a hearing is scheduled to decide the case. A person who is caught trying to avoid paying duty is fined. When customs violations occur, officers must file detailed reports and often later appear as witnesses in court.

CBP agriculture specialists inspect agricultural and related goods that are imported into the United States. They act as agricultural experts at ports of entry to help protect people from agroterrorism and bioterrorism, as well as monitor agricultural imports for diseases and harmful pests.

CBP officers and CBP agriculture specialists cooperate with special agents for the Federal Bureau of Investigation (FBI), the Drug Enforcement Administration, the Food and Drug Administration, and other government agencies.

Some of the specialized fields in the Bureau of Customs and Border Protection are as follows:

Customs pilots, who must have a current Federal Aviation Administration (FAA) commercial pilot's license, conduct air surveillance of illegal traffic crossing U.S. borders by air, land, or sea. They apprehend, arrest, and search violators and prepare reports used to prosecute the criminals. They are stationed along the Canadian and Mexican borders as well as along coastal areas. They fly single- and multi-engine planes and helicopters.

Canine enforcement officers train and use dogs to prevent smuggling of all controlled substances as defined by customs laws. These controlled substances include marijuana, narcotics, and dangerous drugs. After undergoing an intensive 15-week basic training course in the National Detector Dog Training Center, where each officer is paired with a dog and assigned to a post, canine enforcement officers work in cooperation with CBP officers to find and seize contraband and arrest smugglers. Canine enforcement officers also use dogs to detect bomb-making materials or other dangerous substances.

Import specialists become technical experts in a particular line of merchandise, such as wine or electronic equipment. They keep up to date on their area of specialization by going to trade shows and importers' places of business. Merchandise for delivery to commercial importers is examined, classified, and appraised by these specialists who must enforce import quotas and trademark laws. They use import quotas and current market values to determine the unit value of the merchandise in order to calculate the amount of money due the government in tariffs. Import specialists routinely question importers, check their lists, and make sure the merchandise matches the description and the list. If they find a violation, they call for a formal inquiry by customs special agents.

Import specialists regularly deal with problems of fraud and violations of copyright and trademark laws. If the importer meets federal requirements, the import specialist issues a permit that authorizes the release of merchandise for delivery. If not, the goods might be seized and sold at public auction. These specialists encourage international trade by authorizing the lowest allowable duties on merchandise.

Customs and border protection chemists form a subgroup of import specialists who protect the health and safety of Americans. They analyze imported merchandise for textile fibers, lead content, narcotics, and presence of explosives or other harmful material. In many cases, the duty collected on imported products depends on the chemist's analysis and subsequent report. Customs chemists often serve as expert witnesses in court. Customs laboratories have specialized instruments that can analyze materials for their chemical components. These machines can determine such things as the amount of sucrose in a beverage, the fiber content of a textile product, the lead oxide content of fine crystal, or the presence of toxic chemicals and prohibited additives.

Criminal investigators, or *special agents,* are plainclothes investigators who make sure that the government obtains revenue on imports and that contraband and controlled substances do not enter or leave the country illegally. They investigate smuggling, criminal fraud, and major cargo thefts. Special agents target professional criminals as well as ordinary tourists who give false information on baggage declarations. Often working undercover, they cooperate with CBP officers and the FBI. Allowed special powers of entry, search, seizure, and arrest, special agents have the broadest powers of search of any law enforcement personnel in the United States. For instance, special agents do not need probable cause or a warrant to justify search or seizure near a border or port of entry. However, in the interior of the United States, probable cause but not a warrant is necessary to conduct a search.

REQUIREMENTS

High School

If you are interested in working for the U.S. Bureau of Customs and Border Protection, you should pursue a well-rounded education in high school. Courses in government, geography and social studies, English, and history will contribute to your understanding of international and domestic legal issues as well as giving you a good general background. If you wish to become a specialist in scientific or investigative aspects of the CBP, courses in the sciences, particularly chemistry, will be necessary and courses in computer science will be helpful. Taking a foreign language, especially Spanish, will also help prepare you for this career.

Postsecondary Training

Applicants to CBP must be U.S. citizens and at least 21 years of age. They must have earned at least a high school diploma, but applicants with college degrees are preferred. Applicants are required to have three years of general work experience involving contact with the public or four years of college.

Like all federal employees, applicants to CBP must pass a physical examination, undergo a security check, and pass a written test. Entrance-level appointments are at grades GS-5 and GS-7, depending on the level of education or work experience.

New CBP officers participate in a rigorous training program that includes 10 days of pre-academy orientation, 12 weeks of basic training at the U.S. Customs Explorer Academy, In-Port Training (a combination of on-the-job, computer-based, and classroom training), and Advanced Proficiency Training. CBP agricultural specialists receive specialized training from the U.S. Department of Agriculture.

Other Requirements

Applicants must be in good physical condition, be emotionally and mentally stabile, and demonstrate the ability to correctly apply regulations or instructional material and make clear, concise oral or written reports.

EXPLORING

There are several ways for you to learn about the various positions available at CBP. You can read *CBP Today* (http://www.customs.ustreas.gov/xp/cgov/toolbox/publications), the official employee newsletter of the United States Bureau of Customs and Border Protection, to learn more about customs work. You can also talk with people employed as customs workers, consult your high school counselors, or contact local labor union organizations and offices for additional information. Information on federal government jobs is available from offices of the state employment service, area offices of the U.S. Office of Personnel Management, and Federal Job Information Centers throughout the country.

Another great way to learn more about this career is to participate in the CBP Explorer Program. CBP Explorers receive practical and

A customs official and a drug-sniffing dog inspect luggage from an international flight. *(Billy L. Mason, U.S. Customs and Border Protection)*

hands-on training in law enforcement and criminal justice fields. Applicants must be between the ages of 14 and 21 and have at least a C grade point average in high school or college. Participation in this program is also an excellent starting point for entry into the field. After one year in the program, Explorers can apply to the U.S. Customs Explorer Academy.

EMPLOYERS

The Bureau of Customs and Border Protection is the sole employer of customs workers.

STARTING OUT

Applicants may enter the various occupations of the Bureau of Customs and Border Protection by applying to take the appropriate civil service examinations. Interested applicants should note the age, citizenship, and experience requirements previously described and realize that they will undergo a background check and a drug test. If hired, applicants will receive exacting, on-the-job training.

ADVANCEMENT

All CBP workers have the opportunity to advance through a special system of promotion from within. Although they enter at the GS-5 or GS-7 level, after one year they may compete for promotion to supervisory positions or simply to positions at a higher grade level in the agency. The journeyman level is grade GS-11. Supervisory positions are available on a competitive basis.

EARNINGS

Entry-level positions at GS-5 began at a base annual pay of $24,075 in 2004, and entry at GS-7 started at $29,821 per year. Most CBP officers are at the GS-11 position, which had a base annual salary of $44,136 in 2004. Supervisory positions beginning at GS-12 started at $52,899 in 2004. Federal employees in certain cities receive locality pay in addition to their salaries in order to offset the higher cost of living in those areas. Locality pay generally adds from 8.64 percent to 19.04 percent to the base salary. Certain CBP workers are also entitled to receive Law Enforcement Availability Pay, which adds another 25 percent to their salaries. All federal workers receive annual cost-of-living salary increases. Federal workers enjoy generous benefits, including health and life insurance, pension plans, and holiday, sick leave, and vacation pay.

WORK ENVIRONMENT

The customs territory of the United States is divided into nine regions that include the 50 states, the District of Columbia, Puerto Rico, and the U.S. Virgin Islands. In these regions there are 317 ports of entry along land and sea borders. CBP workers may be assigned to any of these ports or to overseas work at airports, seaports, waterfronts, border stations, customs houses, or the U.S. Bureau of Customs and Border Protection headquarters in Washington, D.C. They are able to request assignments in certain localities and usually receive them when possible.

A typical work schedule is eight hours a day, five days a week, but CBP officers and related employees often work overtime or long into the night. United States entry and exit points must be supervised 24 hours a day, which means that workers rotate night shifts and weekend duty. CBP officers are sometimes assigned to one-person border points at remote locations, where they may perform immigration and agricultural inspections in addition to regular duties. They often risk physical injury from criminals violating customs regulations.

OUTLOOK

Employment at the Bureau of Customs and Border Protection is steady work that is not affected by changes in the economy. With the increased emphasis on law enforcement, especially the deterrence of terrorism, but also the detection of illegally imported drugs and pornography and the prevention of exports of sensitive high-technology items, the prospects for steady employment in the CBP are likely to grow and remain high. The U.S. Department of Labor predicts employment for police and detectives, a category including CBP officers, to grow faster than the average through 2012.

FOR MORE INFORMATION

For career information and to view a short video about CBP officers, visit the CBP website.
U.S. Customs and Border Protection
Department of Homeland Security
1300 Pennsylvania Avenue, NW
Washington, DC 20229
Tel: 202-354-1000
http://www.customs.ustreas.gov

Flight Attendants

OVERVIEW

Flight attendants are responsible for the safety and comfort of airline passengers from the time of boarding to disembarkment. They are trained to respond to emergencies and passenger illnesses. Flight attendants are required on almost all national and international commercial flights. There are approximately 104,000 flight attendants employed in the United States.

HISTORY

Although the first commercial passenger flights occurred as early as 1911, early airplane flights were not very comfortable. Airplanes were unstable, relatively small, and could not achieve very high altitudes. It was also difficult to operate passenger service at a profit. In the United States, the commercial aviation industry did not take off until the Kelly Air Mail Act of 1925, which encouraged the growth of the first commercial airlines. For many years, commercial airlines prospered because of profits from their airmail business. The government, in an effort to encourage passenger travel, offered airlines subsidies to lower the price of passenger tickets.

Concerns about the safety of airplanes kept many people from flying. In 1926, however, the Air Commerce Act, which established regulations and requirements for pilots and airlines and also defined an air-traffic system, improved consumer confidence in the airline industry. The famous flight of Charles Lindbergh the following year did much to promote public excitement about flying. Improvements such as stronger engines, better radio and navigational aids, and weather forecasting techniques were making flights safer. An important advancement in commercial air travel came with the development of the pressurized cabin. This meant that passengers could fly unaffected by the thin air of higher altitudes. As more people began to fly, the airlines sought ways to make flights even safer, more comfortable, and more enjoyable for the passenger. United Airlines was the first to offer special service to passengers in flight. In 1930, it hired graduate nurses to tend to passengers' comfort and needs. They were called *stewardesses*, after the similar position on cruise ships. Soon after, other airlines added stewardesses to their flights as well. At first, stewardesses performed many functions for the airlines, often acting as mechanics, refueling airplanes, loading passenger luggage and equipment necessary for the flight, as well as cleaning the interior of the airplane. But as airplanes grew larger and the numbers of passengers increased, these positions were filled by specialized personnel, and the stewardesses' responsibilities were devoted to the passengers. Stewardesses also began preparing and serving meals and drinks during flights.

The increasing growth and regulation of the airline industry brought still more duties for the flight attendant. Flight attendants began to instruct passengers on proper safety procedures, and they were required to make certain that safety factors were met before takeoff.

In the early years, most flight attendants were women, and the airlines often required that they remain unmarried in order to retain their jobs. Airlines also instituted age, height, and weight restrictions. Flight attendants were expected to provide a glamorous and pleasant image for airlines. During this time, employee turnover was very high. However, as the role of the flight attendant became more important and as regulations required them to perform more safety-oriented tasks, the image of the flight attendant changed as well. Because training flight attendants was expensive, the airlines began to offer better benefits and other incentives and removed some of their employee restrictions. Experience was also rewarded with higher pay, better benefits, and seniority privileges given according to the number of years worked. More and more flight attendants were making a career with the airlines. The introduction of Federal Aviation Administration (FAA) regulations requiring at least one flight attendant for every 50 passengers provided even greater growth and job security to this career.

Today, flight attendants fill more positions than any other airline occupation. The 104,000 flight attendants play a vital role in maintaining the safety and comfort in the skies. Many airlines are easing still more of their restrictions, such as age and weight limitations, as the role of the flight attendant has changed to require special training and skills.

THE JOB

Flight attendants perform a variety of preflight and in-flight duties. At least one hour before takeoff, they attend a briefing session with the rest of the flight crew; carefully check flight supplies, emergency life jackets, oxygen masks, and other passenger safety equipment; and see that the passenger cabins are neat, orderly, and furnished with pillows and blankets. They also check the plane galley to see that food and beverages to be served are on board and that the galley is secure for takeoff.

Attendants welcome the passengers on the flight and check their tickets as they board the plane. They show the passengers where to store briefcases and other small parcels, direct them to their cabin section for seating, and help them put their coats and carry-on luggage in overhead compartments. They often give special attention to elderly or disabled passengers and those traveling with small children.

Before takeoff, a flight attendant speaks to the passengers as a group, usually over a loudspeaker. He or she welcomes the passengers and gives the names of the crew and flight attendants, as well as weather, altitude, and safety information. As required by federal law, flight attendants demonstrate the use of lifesaving equipment and safety procedures and check to make sure all passenger seatbelts are fastened before takeoff.

Upon takeoff and landing and during any rough weather, flight attendants routinely check to make sure passengers are wearing their safety belts properly and have their seats in an upright position. They may distribute reading materials to passengers and answer any questions regarding flight schedules, weather, or the geographic terrain over which the plane is passing. Sometimes they call attention to points of interest that can be seen from the plane. They observe passengers during the flight to ensure their personal comfort and assist anyone who becomes airsick or nervous.

During some flights, attendants serve prepared breakfasts, lunches, dinners, or between-meal refreshments. They are responsible for certain clerical duties, such as filling out passenger reports and issuing reboarding passes. They keep the passenger cabins neat and comfortable during flights. Attendants serving on international flights may provide customs and airport information and sometimes translate flight information or passenger instructions into a foreign language. Most flight attendants work for commercial airlines. A small number, however, work on private airplanes owned and operated by corporations or private companies.

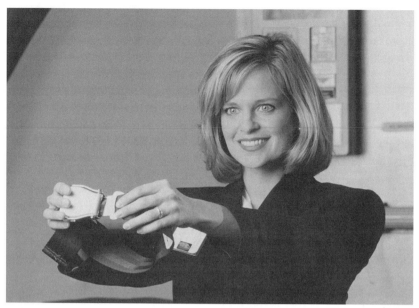

A flight attendant demonstrates proper seatbelt usage to passengers. *(Photo Disc)*

REQUIREMENTS

High School

Flight attendants need to have at least a high school education. A broad education is important to allow flight attendants to cope with the variety of situations they will encounter on the job. Beginning foreign language studies in high school will open up the possibility of working on international flights later.

Postsecondary Training

Applicants with college-level education are often given preference in employment. Business training and experience working with the public are also assets. Attendants employed by international airlines are usually required to be able to converse in a foreign language.

Most large airline companies maintain their own training schools for flight attendants. Training programs may last from four to seven weeks. Some smaller airlines send their applicants to the schools run by the bigger airlines. A few colleges and schools offer flight attendant training, but these graduates may still be required to complete an airline's training program.

Airline training programs usually include classes in company operations and schedules, flight regulations and duties, first aid, grooming, emergency operations and evacuation procedures, flight terminology, and other types of job-related instruction. Flight attendants also receive 12 to 14 hours of additional emergency and passenger procedures training each year. Trainees for international flights are given instruction on customs and visa regulations and are taught procedures for terrorist attacks. Near the end of the training period, trainees are taken on practice flights, in which they perform their duties under supervision.

An on-the-job probationary period, usually six months, follows training school. During this time, experienced attendants pay close attention to the performance, aptitudes, and attitudes of the new attendants. After this period, new attendants serve as reserve personnel and fill in for attendants who are ill or on vacation. While on call, these reserve attendants must be available to work on short notice.

Other Requirements

Airlines in the United States require flight attendants to be U.S. citizens, have permanent resident status, or have valid work visas. In general, applicants must be at least 18 to 21 years old, although some airlines have higher minimum age requirements. They should be at least five feet, two inches tall in order to reach overhead compartments, and their weight should be in proportion to their height.

Airlines are particularly interested in employing people who are intelligent, poised, resourceful, and able to work in a tactful manner with the public. Flight attendants must have excellent health, good vision, and the ability to speak clearly. Young people who are interested in this occupation need to have a congenial temperament, a pleasant personality, and the desire to serve the public. They must be able to think clearly and logically, especially in emergency situations, and they must be able to follow instructions working as team members of flight crews.

EXPLORING

Opportunities for experience in this occupation are almost nonexistent until you have completed flight attendant training school. You may explore this occupation by talking with flight attendants or people in airline personnel offices. Airline companies and private training schools publish many brochures describing the work of flight attendants and send them out upon request.

Any part-time job in customer service, such as food service, hospitality, or retail sales, would be a good introduction to the kind of work flight attendants do. You might also try volunteering for jobs that require people skills, such as diplomacy, listening, helping, and explaining.

EMPLOYERS

Approximately 104,000 professionally trained flight attendants are employed in the United States. Commercial airlines employ the vast majority of all flight attendants, most of whom are stationed in the major cities that serve as their airline's home base. A very small number of flight attendants work on company-owned or private planes.

STARTING OUT

Individuals who are interested in becoming flight attendants should apply directly to the personnel divisions of airline companies. The names and locations of these companies may be obtained by writing to the Air Transport Association of America. Addresses of airline personnel division offices can also be obtained from almost any airline office or ticket agency. Some major airlines have personnel recruiting teams that travel throughout the United States interviewing prospective flight attendants. Airline company offices can provide interested people with information regarding these recruitment visits, which are sometimes announced in newspaper advertisements in advance.

ADVANCEMENT

A number of advancement opportunities are open to flight attendants. They may advance to supervisory positions such as *first flight attendant* (sometimes known as the *flight purser* or the *supervising flight attendant*) or become an instructor or airline recruitment representative. They may also have the opportunity to move into the position of *chief attendant,* representing all flight attendants in a particular division or area. Although the rate of turnover in this field was once high, more people are making careers as flight attendants, and competition for available supervisory jobs is very high.

Many flight attendants who no longer qualify for flight duty because of health or other factors move into other jobs with the airlines. These jobs may include reservation agent, ticket agent, or personnel recruiter. They may also work in the public relations, sales, air transportation, dispatch, or communications divisions. Trained flight attendants may also find similar employment in other transportation or hospitality industries such as luxury cruise ship lines.

EARNINGS

Beginning flight attendants earned a median salary of $14,847 a year in 2002, according to the Association of Flight Attendants. Median annual earnings of all flight attendants were $43,140 in 2002, according to the *Occupational Outlook Handbook*. The middle 50 percent earned between $31,660 and $66,260. Salaries ranged from less than $20,890 to more than $91,050. Wage and work schedule requirements are established by union contract. Most flight attendants are members of the Transport Workers Union of America or the Association of Flight Attendants.

Flight attendants are limited to a specific number of flying hours. In general, they work approximately 65 to 85 hours of scheduled flying time and an additional 50 hours of ground duties each month. They receive extra compensation for overtime and night flights. Flight attendants on international flights customarily earn higher salaries than those on domestic flights. Most airlines give periodic salary increases until a maximum pay ceiling is reached. Flight assignments are often based on seniority, with the most senior flight attendants having their choice of flight times and destinations.

Airlines usually pay flight attendants in training either living expenses or a training salary. Companies usually pay flight attendants' expenses such as food, ground transportation, and overnight accommodations while they are on duty or away from home base. Some airlines may require first-year flight attendants to furnish their own uniforms, but most companies supply them.

Fringe benefits include paid sick leave and vacation time, free or reduced air travel rates for attendants and their families, and, in some cases, group hospitalization and life insurance plans and retirement benefits.

WORK ENVIRONMENT

Flight attendants are usually assigned to a home base in a major city or large metropolitan area. These locations include New York, Chicago, Boston, Miami, Los Angeles, San Francisco, and St. Louis. Some airlines assign attendants on a rotation system to home bases, or they may give preference to the requests of those with rank and seniority on bids for certain home bases. Those with the longest records of service may be given the most desirable flights and schedules.

Flight attendants need to be flexible in their work schedules, mainly because commercial airlines maintain operations 24 hours a day throughout the entire year. They may be scheduled to work nights, weekends, and on holidays, and they may find that some of their allotted time off occurs away from home between flights. They are often away from home for several days at a time. They work long days, but over a year's time, a flight attendant averages about 156 days off, compared with 96 days off for the average office worker.

The work flight attendants perform may be physically demanding in some respects. For most of the flight, they are usually on their feet servicing passengers' needs, checking safety precautions, and, in many cases, serving meals and beverages. Working with the public all day can be draining. Flight attendants are the most visible employees of the airline, and they must be courteous to everyone, even passengers who are annoying or demanding. There is a certain degree of risk involved in any type of flight work. Flight attendants may suffer minor injuries as they perform their duties in a moving aircraft. They may suffer from irregular sleeping and eating patterns, dealing with stressful passengers, working in a pressurized environment, and breathing recycled air. Flight attendants also face risk of injury or death from hijackings. Since September 11, 2001, airlines and the Department of Transportation have implemented comprehensive security measures and upgrades to ensure the safety of travelers and industry workers.

The combination of free time and the opportunity to travel are benefits that many flight attendants enjoy. For those who enjoy helping and working with people, being a flight attendant may be a rewarding career.

OUTLOOK

The U.S. Department of Labor predicts that employment opportunities for flight attendants will grow about as fast as the average through 2012. The terrorist attacks of 2001 had a great impact on the airline industry and several thousand flight attendants were laid off. The airline industry predicts a slow economic recovery as passengers gradually return to the skies. Economic and political conditions are likely to affect all airline employees over the next few years.

Even in the best of times, finding employment as a flight attendant is highly competitive, and since some job restrictions at airlines have been abolished, the once high rate of turnover for flight attendants has declined. Even though the number of job openings is expected to grow, airlines receive thousands of applications each year. Students interested in this career will have a competitive advantage if they have at least two years of college and prior work experience in customer relations or public contact. Courses in business, psychology, sociology, geography, speech, communications, first aid and emergency medical techniques such as CPR, and knowledge of foreign languages and cultures will make the prospective flight attendant more attractive to the airlines.

FOR MORE INFORMATION

For industry and statistical information, as well as to read the Airline Handbook *online, visit ATAA's website.*
Air Transport Association of America
1301 Pennsylvania Avenue, NW, Suite 1100
Washington, DC 20004-1707
Tel: 202-626-4000
Email: ata@airlines.org
http://www.airlines.org

For information on union membership, contact
Association of Flight Attendants
1275 K Street, NW, 5th Floor
Washington, DC 20005
Tel: 202-712-9799
Email: afatalk@afanet.org
http://www.afanet.org/afa

For information on aviation safety, statistics, and regulations, contact
Federal Aviation Administration
800 Independence Avenue, SW, Room 810
Washington, DC 20591
Tel: 202-366-4000
http://www.faa.gov

This website offers information on careers and job issues and links to discussion forums and other aviation-related sites.
Flight Attendants.org
http://www.flightattendants.org

Flight Instructors

QUICK FACTS

School Subjects
Mathematics
Physics

Personal Skills
Leadership/management
Technical/scientific

Work Environment
Indoors and outdoors
Primarily multiple
  locations

Minimum Education Level
Some postsecondary training

Salary Range
$12,300 to $40,530 to
  $75,000+

Certification or Licensing
Required by all states

Outlook
About as fast as the
  average

DOT
097, 099, 196

GOE
05.04.01, 11.02.02

NOC
2271

O*NET-SOC
25-1194.00, 53-2011.00

OVERVIEW

Flight instructors are pilots who use their experience, knowledge, joy of flying, and ability to explain complex subjects to teach students how to fly aircraft. Flight instructors give classroom as well as hands-on flying instruction to their students. Topics covered include aerodynamics, navigation, instrument reading, aircraft control techniques, and federal aviation regulations. They may teach at flight schools, for airlines, in the military, or work as self-employed instructors. There are approximately 109,000 flight instructors working in the United States.

HISTORY

People have been interested in figuring out how to fly for hundreds of years. Before the 20th century, however, attempts at flying were generally based on self-taught methods and self-experimentation. Flying enthusiasts generally studied the efforts of others and created their own aircraft (or what they hoped would be aircraft). In 1903, Orville and Wilbur Wright completed their first flight with a powered flying machine and began the period of modern aviation. In 1906, Alberto Santos-Dumont completed the first flight in Europe, and in 1909 Louis Blériot made the first flight across the English Channel, flying from France to England in slightly over 30 minutes.

By the 1920s the commercial benefits of airplanes—flying mail, goods, and people—had become apparent and more and more people were interested in using flight and learning to fly. The federal government became involved in regulating the aviation field with the passing of the Air Commerce Act in 1926. With this act, the Department of Commerce took responsibility for such actions as issuing and enforcing air traffic rules, setting standards for pilot certification (licensing), and establishing airways. A significant development in teaching methods occurred a few years later, when in 1929 Edwin Link invented the Link trainer. The Link trainer, a flight simulator, was a ground-operated machine that simulated flying conditions and reduced some of the time, expense, and danger of training new pilots. Advances in flight were spurred by both World War I and World War II, when the military use of aircraft became a major focus of the aviation industry. The military also provided an environment for training pilots, and other crew members, in an organized and uniform process.

In the meantime, government oversight of the field continued to grow, and in 1938 the regulation of aviation was transferred from the Department of Commerce to a new agency—the Civil Aeronautics Authority. This organization eventually grew into what is now the Federal Aviation Administration (FAA). The FAA is responsible for setting and enforcing rules of air safety, traffic, and education. The days of trying to figure out how to fly on your own are gone; today's pilots must complete extensive training and education before the FAA grants flight instructor certification.

THE JOB

Simply put, the job of a flight instructor combines both the work of a pilot and the work of a teacher. In order to teach others how to fly, flight instructors must first become pilots themselves, learning how to command an aircraft in flight as well as taking care of responsibilities on the ground. Although flight instructors fly with students, it is the instructor who is ultimately responsible for making sure all appropriate preflight, in-flight, and afterlanding procedures are followed. Therefore, like any pilot, instructors must know how to complete such preflight duties as making sure the aircraft is properly maintained and has the right amount of fuel, preparing a flight plan and knowing the latest weather conditions, and testing the airplane's instruments and controls. In flight, the instructor's piloting duties include monitoring the airplane's systems, paying attention to weather conditions, and making sure there is communication with air traffic control. Some of the afterlanding duties instructors must know how to complete are shutting down the airplane, explaining any problems to the maintenance crew, and updating their flight logbooks.

In addition to all the skill, knowledge, and experience needed to complete these and other pilot tasks, instructors have teaching responsibilities. William Jones, an assistant chief flight instructor at the Institute of Aviation, University of Illinois-Urbana Champaign, emphasizes that only those who want to teach will be good at this work. He notes, "There's nothing sadder than an instructor whose heart isn't into instructing because then the flight student is the one who really loses out." Flight instructors may work on their own, offering private lessons or at ground schools that are at an airport, part of a major airline, in the military, or, like William Jones, part of a university. Their teaching duties include deciding what classes to offer, making a syllabus, scheduling class times, and picking out the textbooks and other materials that the students will need. Instructors must know current federal aviation regulations so that they can teach correct rules to their students. Flight instructors should also be up to date on the latest teaching technologies available. Computer-based programs and flight simulators, for example, are often used in flight instruction, and instructors should be able to make use of these resources.

Flight instructors, like other kinds of teachers, spend time outside of the classroom preparing for what they will teach. They may write lectures, make PowerPoint presentations, arrange for demonstrations of equipment, and grade tests or otherwise keep track of each student's progress. Subjects that instructors cover during class meetings include principles of aerodynamics, the national airspace system, navigation, meteorology, instrument reading, and proper use of radio communications. They also demonstrate how to use equipment and discuss the functions of parts of an airplane, such as rudders, flaps, and elevators. Another important classroom activity is overseeing students' use of flight simulators. A flight simulator is made to look and feel like the cockpit of an airplane, with instrument panels and a pilot's seat. In the simulator students can practice maneuvers such as taking off, flying, and landing. Instructors are able to monitor a student's actions while in the simulator, and they can use a control panel to change conditions during the student's simulated flight. This helps students develop skills they will need when faced with changing conditions in real-life flying situations. After a session in the flight simulator, the instructor and student review the student's actions and discuss what was done well, what needs improvement, and how to work on these areas.

Taking students on training flights is another important part of a flight instructor's work. Aircraft that are designed for training have two sets of controls and a cockpit arranged so that the student and instructor sit either side by side or one in front of the other. Because there are two sets of controls, the instructor can observe the student's flying but also be able to take back control of the plane if the student needs help. During training flights, instructors can show students how to handle the plane in different situations, how to use instruments like the altimeter and vertical speed indicator, and how to do maneuvers that may help the student during a dangerous situation in the future. Safety is a top priority for instructors and they may take students through emergency situations, such as a stall, to teach them how to react. Flight instructors also teach students how to maintain a flight logbook. Each student must record information about the flights he or she makes, such as what was done on the flight, how long the flight took, and the flight's distance. In addition, instructors need to keep their own "teacher's logbook" with information on each student. These logbooks must be kept by instructors for at least three years after they have had a student.

Before flight instructors can let students make their first solo flight, the students must get a medical certificate (certifying they are in good health) and an instructor-endorsed student pilot certificate. In order to get the student pilot certificate, the student must pass a test given by the flight instructor. This test will have questions about FAA rules as well as questions about the model and make of the aircraft the student will fly. If the student passes the test and the instructor feels the student is prepared to make a solo flight, the instructor will sign—or endorse—the student pilot certificate and the student logbook. The flight instructor's work isn't done yet, though; they continue to work with students until the students complete all their training and get their FAA pilot's certificate (sometimes called a license).

Not all students are beginners. Some students are already pilots who want to become certified as another type of pilot or for another type of aircraft. Someone with a recreational pilot's certificate, for example, may want to get a private pilot's certificate. Someone with a private pilot's certificate may want to get a commercial pilot's certificate. Someone else may want to earn a certificate for flying multi-engine planes. Flight instructors are only allowed to teach the categories for which they are already certified. Because of this, instructors are often students themselves, spending their spare time learning how to operate different aircraft and getting various certifications. William Jones has had just such a career. He explains, "I started out in gliders in 1973 and since then have flown and instructed in everything from them through tactical military jets. Therefore, I now have 31 years of flying experience in quite a variety of aircraft."

Many instructors see this need to expand on their flying skills and certifications as an opportunity for both professional achievement and personal satisfaction.

REQUIREMENTS

High School
Remember that if you want to work as a flight instructor, you'll have to become a pilot first. So take classes in high school that will prepare you for college. Chemistry, physics, algebra, geometry, and other advanced science and math classes are important to take. Since a career in this field demands extensive use of technology, be sure to take computer courses. To help you develop your teaching skills, take English or communications classes—these will improve your writing and speaking abilities. You may also want to take acting or drama classes as well as psychology. Again, these classes should help you with teaching skills such as commanding an audience and learning to understand others.

Postsecondary Training
Although the FAA does not require flight instructors to have a particular degree, a college education is highly recommended. You may want to attend a university with a specialized aviation program, such as the Institute of Aviation at the University of Illinois-Urbana Champaign, where William Jones works. If you prefer, though, you can take a broader course of study at any college. Continue your math and science studies, taking courses such as aerodynamics, physics, and college algebra. Classes in geography and meteorology are also helpful. If your school offers classes in the fundamentals of teaching or instruction, take these as well. And, naturally, keep up with your computer skills. Another option is to get your pilot training in the military, and you may want to contact your local recruiting offices for more information.

If you do not attend a specialized aviation program or get your training in the military, you will need to get flight instruction, either from an instructor who offers private lessons or through a flight school, also known as pilot school. The FAA provides information on pilot schools; visit http://www.faa.gov to find out more. As you learn how to fly, be aware of your school experience as well. What does your instructor do that you like or find helpful? Do you like the size of the school and the equipment there? After all, answers to questions like these may help you determine where you want to work eventually as an instructor.

Certification and Licensing

To become a flight instructor, you will need to get FAA flight-instructor certification. To do this, you must have a commercial pilot's certification for the kind of aircraft (single engine, multi-engine, instrument, and so on) that matches the flight instructor rating (designation) you want to have. You must have accumulated a certain amount of flying time and have your logbook properly endorsed. You must have completed training that covered topics such as evaluation of student flight performance, lesson planning, and how to properly instruct on stall awareness, spin entry, spins, and spin-recovery methods. In addition, you will need to pass a test with written and oral sections as well as a flight test. Certification renewal is on a two-year basis.

The National Association of Flight Instructors offers several professional certifications, including the master certified flight instructor and the master certified flight instructor-aerobatic. These certifications are voluntary and demonstrate commitment to the profession. To earn these, an instructor must meet certain requirements, such as being a member of the association, having FAA flight instructor certification, and completing a certain amount of continuing education credits or activities.

Other Requirements

You must pass a physical exam and be certified fit to fly. Naturally, anyone controlling an aircraft needs to have good vision. So you must have eyesight of 20/20 or better in each eye, although you can wear glasses or contact lenses to get this. Good hearing is also a requirement. In addition to physical and intellectual requirements, flight instructors need to be calm, have good judgment, be able to deal well with people, and, of course, have a love of flying. William Jones also believes character and principles are part of the job. He advises, "If you do instruct, then ethics and integrity demand that you provide your student with the best instruction you can provide. The only way we can develop competent future aviators is by providing superior instruction, motivation, and mentoring."

EXPLORING

You can explore aspects of this field while you are still in high school. Begin by reading aviation magazines as well as more complex materials with FAA rules and other information. The FAA publishes study materials covering topics such as aviation weather, aeronautical knowledge, and weight and balance. Its website has information on how to get these study guides. You can also begin developing radio skills, which you will need as a pilot, by learning to use a ham radio.

Although you must be at least 16 to get a student pilot certificate for solo flying, you can start taking flying lessons even if you're younger. This will allow you to see how much you enjoy the flying experience as well as let you work with a flight instructor and, in that way, get a close up view of the instructor's job. If you can't afford lessons, you can still meet and interview a local flight instructor to get information about this type of work.

Another fun thing to do is to go to air shows, which are frequently held during the summers. Check for shows or "fly-ins" in your area or plan a trip to one. The Experimental Aircraft Association (EAA) holds one of the largest such fly-ins each summer in Oshkosh, Wisconsin, as well as other regional fly-ins across the country. At these shows you can meet other flying enthusiasts, see every kind of aircraft from homebuilts (those built by the pilots themselves) to sophisticated military aircraft, attend workshops, and watch flying demonstrations. The EAA also offers Air Academy Aviation Camps for those ages 10 to 18 as well as weekend "camps" for adults. For more information about these opportunities, visit http://www.eaa.org.

EMPLOYERS

Flight instructors who are in the military are employed by the U.S. government. In the civilian world, flight instructors are typically employed by flight schools or they may work independently, offering lessons on their own. Some instructors may begin by working at an established flight school but have the goal of eventually running their own school. Flight schools are located all across the country, and many airports have them. The warmer months of the year tend to be busiest for flight instructors because this is when it is easiest to take beginners out for training flights. Of course, flight instructors working in locations where the weather is fairly warm all year usually do not experience such fluctuations. Schools are classified as FAA-approved or nonapproved. This is based on factors such as the amount and type of equipment, personnel, and facilities the school has. Many nonapproved schools offer excellent training but do not seek FAA approval simply because of their smaller size or other factors. Approximately 109,000 flight instructors are employed in the United States, but because some flight instructors combine this work with other work, such as piloting chartered flights, it is difficult to determine the exact number of these workers.

STARTING OUT

Since pilots need to log flying time as one requirement for gaining different certifications, a number of people choose to begin their careers as flight instructors. Then as they gain time and experience they may move on to other positions, such as pilot at a major airline, which is their ultimate goal. Some flight instructors, like William Jones, start out with careers as military pilots and then become instructors later in their professional lives. Another way to gain entry into the field is through connections made at flight school. In fact, some students who have impressed their instructors may be offered a job there. William Jones notes that the Institute of Aviation has "permanent long-term instructors like myself . . . blended with young instructors fresh from our program, which allows for an employment track for our best graduates."

ADVANCEMENT

Advancement often depends on the individual's goals. Some instructors may want to advance to the point of running their own schools. An instructor working at a small airport school may want to move on to work at a large school in a metropolitan area or at a school that is part of a university. And other instructors may simply want to increase the number of students they teach. No matter what the goal, however, the best way to make any type of advancement in this field is by gaining as much personal flying experience as possible and becoming certified to pilot a variety of aircraft. It is extremely important for those in this career to keep up with new technologies, regulations, and other developments. Only those who are willing to continuously challenge themselves to increase their skills and knowledge will advance the most.

EARNINGS

"With the huge impact flight instructors have on the overall advances and safety of aviation, it's really sad that instructors are at the low end of the aviation pay scale," William Jones says. "That's a major reason many great instructors leave the profession to move on to other flying opportunities." So why stay in the profession? Jones explains, "Flight instructors are a lot like school teachers—the hours may be long and pay may be low, but the personal satisfaction gained from the job is what keeps many of us in the business."

Flight instructors' earnings vary based on factors such as the size and type of employer, the type of aircraft used, and the amount of experience the instructor has. According to the FAA, instructors working at flight schools may earn from $12,300 to $40,530 a year. A few flight instructors with extensive experience and working for major airlines may earn as much as $75,000 or more a year. Instructors who work independently (that is, are self-employed) typically charge an hourly fee, which may be approximately between $30 and $50 an hour. Their yearly income, though, depends on the number of students they have and the amount of time they are actually able to spend teaching.

The benefits a flight instructor receives depend on the employer. For example, those working at colleges or universities typically receive the same health insurance, paid vacation time, and retirement plans as other teachers there. At major airlines, instructors also typically get health insurance, paid vacation and sick time, and retirement plans. In addition, they may get stock options through the company. Those working at small nonapproved schools may get a minimum of health insurance and little or no retirement plan. And instructors who are self-employed do not receive any benefits.

WORK ENVIRONMENT

Flight instructors work in classrooms and in aircraft, and they must be comfortable working with computers, machines, and people. In order to accommodate their students' schedules, many instructors hold classes in the evenings or on weekends. FAA rules limit the number of hours per day that a flight instructor can spend giving in-flight instruction; however, instructors can spend as much time as they want doing classroom work. On average, instructors work between 40 and 50 hours a week. Those who work at small schools or independently may spend part of their time teaching and part of their time doing other flying jobs to supplement their income.

Instructors must be able to deal with stressful situations in the air, including mechanical problems, sudden changes in weather, and students' fears or mistakes. On the other hand, as William Jones points out, flight instructors can enjoy working in a positive environment: "What other job can provide the joy and sense of accomplishment you and your student will both feel when they make their first solo flight?"

OUTLOOK

The U.S. Department of Labor estimates that job growth for all types of pilots will grow at an average rate through 2012. However, the department also notes that the growth rate depends a great deal on both the pilot's specific occupation and the overall condition of the economy. When the economy is bad, fewer people will be able to afford such expenses as flying lessons. With a decrease in student enrollment, flight schools will hire fewer instructors. Additionally, instructors who are working will be more likely to keep those jobs than to move into other positions, such as airline pilot, and make way for new flight instructors.

Of course, another factor influencing job growth is terrorist activities. After the terrorist attacks of September 11, 2001, the entire air transportation industry experienced an enormous economic downturn, and many workers, including pilots, lost their jobs. However, as people have become more confident about the safety of flying, and as the country's economy in general has improved, the airline industry has begun to recover. Naturally, another terrorist attack involving airplanes would again affect this field. Nevertheless, many professionals are hopeful about the future. William Jones sums up his feelings by saying, "We just hope the good times outweigh the bad."

FOR MORE INFORMATION

For information about fly-ins, various aircraft, and membership, visit the website or contact
Experimental Aircraft Association
EAA Aviation Center
PO Box 3086
Oshkosh, WI 54903-3086
Tel: 920-426-4800
http://www.eaa.org

For information on its aviation camps, contact
EAA Air Academy
PO Box 3086
Oshkosh, WI 54903-3086
Tel: 888-322-3229
http://www.eaa.org/education/airacademy.html

For more information about the history of the FAA, pilot schools, and certification, contact
Federal Aviation Administration
800 Independence Avenue, SW, Room 810
Washington, DC 20591
Tel: 202-366-4000
http://www.faa.gov

For information on professional certifications, contact
National Association of Flight Instructors
Kermit Weeks Hangar
1145 West 20 Avenue
Oshkosh, WI 54902-6649
Tel: 920-426-6801
http://www.NAFInet.org

INTERVIEW

William Jones is an assistant chief flight instructor at the Institute of Aviation, University of Illinois at Urbana-Champaign. He has 31 years of experience in the military and civilian aviation industries. He spoke about the aviation program at the university and aviation careers with the editors of Careers in Focus: Aviation.

Q. Can you give a brief overview of the aviation program at the University of Illinois at Urbana-Champaign?

A. Our aviation program began in 1946 and averages around 300 flight students. Our training fleet consists of 18 Piper Archer aircraft for basic and instrument training, six Piper Arrows for commercial- and flight-instructor training, three multi-engine Piper Seminoles, two Cessna 152s for spin training and flying team competition, two Beechcraft Sundowners for research, plus a variety of single- and multi-engine flight simulators. Our instructional staff averages 25 full-time flight/ground instructors, plus each semester around 20 advanced students teach a few students after receiving their flight instructor certificate. We offer one aviation major in aviation human factors, and about half of our flight students pursue that program. The remainder can receive all the same flight training, but pursue a degree in the field of their choosing. All pertinent information about our program can be found online at http://www.aviation.uiuc.edu.

Q. For what type of jobs does your program prepare students?

A. Our program prepares our students for flight and management careers in commercial, military, or general aviation plus various other aviation-related fields such as the National Transportation Safety Board (NTSB) and state aviation management programs.

Q. What internships opportunities are available to students at your school?

A. Our students have the opportunity to apply for internships with many of the major airlines such as United and American. These are normally unpaid internships, but they normally guarantee the person an interview with that airline at some later date when they meet the flight requirements. Other students have interned with the NTSB.

Another student recently did an internship with AirNet [a company that transports documents at night for the banking industry]; they liked him so much it turned immediately into a full-time paid position. In the past two months, that individual has helped four of our young instructors get full-time flying jobs with AirNet.

Q. What are the most important personal and professional qualities for aviation majors?

A. The two most important personal and professional qualities for aviation majors are integrity coupled with a burning desire to fly. Aviation is unlike any other type of career in that it has to be in your blood. If you can't get excited about being around aircraft then you're in the wrong field. The hazards of aviation can be too great to not be totally committed to it.

Q. What advice would you offer aviation majors as they graduate and look for jobs?

A. The best advice I give our graduates is to get whatever flying job they can to start building time. The answer for eventually getting their dream job is to have flight experience and the only way they can get that is by "building time" via entry-level flying jobs. For many, this is flight instruction, while others find flying jobs such as banner towing, glider towing, flying cancelled checks at night, or flying cargo. Again, the main thing is to fly and to build their pilot-in-command hours on their resume.

Q. What is the current state of the job market for flight instructors and pilots?

A. Aviation can be very cyclic and depending on the times can be extremely fast moving while at other times very stagnant. Pilots need to understand this nature of the business. In 1993 when I retired from the Marine Corps with 4,000 flight hours and every possible rating, I couldn't even get an interview with an airline. Fortunately, I was hired to instruct here at U of I, and 11 years later am still here and extremely happy. On the other hand, in 1996 my 21-year-old son was hired by Continental Express with only 1,400 hours, was upgraded to captain at 23, to captain on regional jets at 24, and then moved up to Continental at 26 and flew as First Officer on 737s until 9/11.

Since then he's been furloughed back to Express and is again flying as a regional jet captain.

Therefore, since 9/11 the industry has been quite stagnant with all the airline furloughs, so our young instructors haven't had any place to move up to and our graduates were having trouble finding any flying jobs for a while. Things are picking up now and our young instructors who have been around for a few years are all moving on now—finally making way for recent graduates to get hired on with our program. So, you can see how the entire aviation food chain is tied to the economy of the major airlines and pilots need to understand this. We just hope the good times outweigh the bad.

Q. What is the future of your program?

A. The future of our professional pilot program (aka pilot training) couldn't be brighter. With an entire fleet of all brand-new Piper aircraft, a new multimillion-dollar training facility, and a continued demand for our program, we should be able to perform our mission of developing leaders for the aviation industry for countless years to come.

Ground Services Workers

OVERVIEW

Ground service workers play a significant role in the aviation process. They ensure the safety, security, and comfort of passengers, oversee the loading and unloading of cargo and baggage, and prepare aircraft for flight. Their level of organization determines how smoothly the flight process will be for passengers and flight crew.

HISTORY

For as long as aircraft have been taking off and landing at airports, there has been a need for ground services workers. But it wasn't until after World War II that the commercial airline industry began to grow and prosper. New airlines emerged to compete for the business of air travelers, and many ground services workers were needed to maintain aircraft, process and transport baggage and cargo, prepare food for flights, refuel planes, and perform countless other tasks. Today, ground services workers play an integral role in the success and efficient functioning of our nation's 540 commercial service airports.

THE JOB

There are many different types of ground service workers. *Air freight agents* oversee the shipment of air freight. They receive shipments and supervise the loading and unloading of freight. *Ramp service workers* are responsible for

QUICK FACTS

School Subjects
Mathematics
Physical education
Technical/shop

Personal Skills
Following instructions
Mechanical/manipulative

Work Environment
Indoors and outdoors
Primarily multiple locations

Minimum Education Level
High school diploma

Salary Range
$10,712 to $25,000 to $37,440

Certification or Licensing
Required for certain positions

Outlook
About as fast as the average

DOT
248, 352, 357, 919

GOE
05.09.01, 05.12.18, 09.01.04, 09.05.03

NOC
6661, 7437

O*NET-SOC
43-5011.00, 53-1011.00, 53-2022.00, 53-7062.03

keeping the exterior of the aircraft in top shape. They wash and polish the plane, touch up paint, and perform other necessary cleaning tasks.

Linepersons meet the arriving aircraft and guide it to an appropriate parking area. They secure the aircraft, check for fluid leaks or changes in tire pressure, and often serve as a greeter to passengers. At smaller facilities, linepersons may also coordinate rental cars, catering, and other services for passengers and employees.

Between flights, *ramp agents* prepare for arriving aircraft by readying the wheellocks, beltloaders (for baggage unloading), and other machinery used for landing and takeoff. Ramp agents also perform maintenance tasks such as spraying de-icing solution on the plane's wings during winter conditions and keeping the landing area free of debris.

Drivers transport supplies, equipment, and people throughout the airport. They include drivers of food trucks, mobile stairs, cleaning equipment, aviation fuel, and other supplies. These workers also drive maintenance specialists and other employees to specified terminals and aircraft in a timely manner.

Cabin service workers clean the inside of the airplane and the cockpit in between flights. These workers, who are also referred to as *aircraft servicers,* replace headrests, fold blankets, and fill seat backs with magazines and safety information. Cabin service workers vacuum, pick up trash, wash windows and bathrooms, and ensure the overall cleanliness of the interior of the plane.

Baggage and air cargo handlers load and unload baggage, air mail, and air express and air cargo shipments for passengers. They must be both careful and precise in the handling and placement of baggage. Handlers must sort and stack baggage in the underside of the airplane, positioning luggage so that different groups of passengers will have access to their luggage at different destinations. Baggage handling involves heavy lifting and is a physically demanding occupation. There is little room for error as a baggage and air cargo handler. *Baggage service agents* assist passengers with delayed, lost, or damaged luggage.

Aircraft fuelers, along with drivers, operate fueling equipment. Fuel truck drivers transport the aviation fuel to the waiting aircraft, and the fueler then climbs onto the wings of the plane with a hose and fills it with fuel. Workers in this occupation need to be agile and able to work under deadline pressure.

Food service workers prepare meals that are served during flights. They follow set recipes to prepare the food, and they make sure they have the correct number of serving dishes for each flight. Food service workers place the food in containers for pickup and also clean soiled dishes. Other food service workers are employed in airport restaurants and bars.

Operations agents ensure that the flight process runs smoothly for both passengers and employees. They keep track of the number of passengers and pieces of luggage. Operations agents communicate information to and from pilots, ground crews, and aircraft fuelers. If a flight is overbooked, operations agents must make decisions to remedy the situation and keep passengers calm.

All ground service workers must be efficient, precise, and timely in their work. Their preparation and attention to detail makes the flight process enjoyable and safe for those aboard the aircraft.

REQUIREMENTS

High School

High school courses that will help prepare you for this career include computer science, mathematics, and shop. Since many of these positions require workers to lift or move heavy loads, taking physical education classes and participating in sports will help you build your physical strength and endurance. If you are interested in the career of air freight agent or operations agent, be sure to take as many business, mathematics, accounting, and computer classes as possible. If your interests lie more in the area of food preparation, classes in family and consumer science and health will help you prepare for work in these careers.

Postsecondary Training

Although most ground services jobs are entry-level and require only a high school diploma (or the equivalent), many airlines like job applicants to have some general postsecondary education.

Certification and Licensing

In most states, airport and other professional drivers must qualify for a commercial driver's license. State motor vehicle departments can provide information on how to qualify for this license. Food service workers are required by law in most states to possess a health certificate and to be examined periodically. These examinations, usually given by the state board of health, make certain that the individual is free from communicable diseases and skin infections. Aircraft fuelers must meet rules and regulations established by the Federal Aviation Administration (FAA). They often satisfy these requirements through employer-administered certification.

Other Requirements

All ground services workers should have good communication and teamwork skills and be able to work quickly. Workers who drive vehicles and ground equipment need to have a valid driver's license. Baggage handlers and ramp agents must be able to lift heavy baggage, cargo, or equipment, as well as operate machinery. Baggage service agents must have excellent people skills in order to deal with passengers who are angry or frustrated by lost or damaged luggage. Fuelers should have a basic aptitude for machinery and equipment. Age requirements for these positions vary by employer, but most require applicants to be at least 18 to 21 years of age.

EXPLORING

One of the best ways to learn about a career in ground services is to talk with a worker in the field. Ask your teacher or guidance counselor to set up an information interview with an aircraft servicer, baggage and cargo handler, or other worker in the field. You can also visit the career section of the FAA website (http://www. faa.gov/education/rlib/career.htm) to read about careers in ground service.

EMPLOYERS

Airlines, airports, and airport service contractors are the primary employers of ground services workers.

STARTING OUT

Employment as a ground services worker is an excellent way to break into the aviation industry. Contact airlines, airports, and airport service contractors directly for possible job leads. These positions are also often listed in the classified sections of newspapers.

ADVANCEMENT

With hard work, dedication, and additional education or training, ground services workers can advance to a variety of managerial and supervisory positions. For example, air freight agents can advance to the position of supervisor of air freight handlers or ramp service planner. Food service workers can become chefs or food service managers. Cabin service workers can advance to positions as drivers, air-

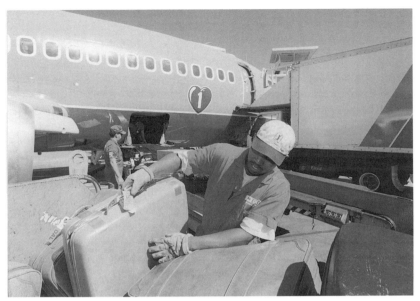

A baggage handler prepares to load luggage onto an airplane.
(Southwest Airlines)

craft fuelers, and baggage and cargo handlers. A very experienced worker who earns a college degree in airport management, business administration, or engineering can become an assistant airport manager or airport manager.

EARNINGS

Salaries for ground services workers vary based on the size and location of the airport and the worker's job description and level of experience. Entry-level workers may initially earn minimum wage. The Federal Aviation Administration reports the following annual salary ranges by profession: air freight agents, $15,000 to $31,000; ramp service workers and linepersons, $14,560 to $31,200; ramp agents, $13,520 to $15,600; aircraft servicers, $12,480 to $14,560; baggage and cargo handlers, $12,480 to $37,440; aircraft fuelers, $16,640 to $20,800; food service workers, $12,480 to $18,720; and operations agents and drivers, $14,560 to $16,640.

Ground services workers receive typical fringe benefits, including medical and dental insurance, life insurance, paid sick and vacation days, and the opportunity to participate in a 401(k) or similar savings plan.

WORK ENVIRONMENT

Ground services areas are typically noisy, hectic, and sometimes dangerous settings as workers go about their duties, luggage and cargo are loaded and unloaded, and heavy equipment and conveyor belts are used to ready an aircraft for flight. Ground services employees often work outdoors in all types of weather. Most ground services workers are required to wear uniforms for security purposes, as well as earplugs and other protective equipment to ensure their safety. Since flights arrive and depart 24 hours a day, seven days a week, ground services workers may be required to work nights and weekends.

OUTLOOK

Employment in the air transportation industry is expected to grow more slowly than the average through 2012, according to the U.S. Department of Labor (USDL). Commercial air travel has decreased as a result of the terrorist attacks of September 11, 2001, creating less need for airport workers. Passenger and cargo traffic is expected to rebound slowly over the next several years. The USDL predicts that employment opportunities will be good for ground services workers, such as baggage handlers and aircraft cleaners, as a result of high turnover in these occupations.

FOR MORE INFORMATION

To read The Airline Handbook, *visit the ATAA website.*
  Air Transport Association of
    America
  1301 Pennsylvania Avenue, NW, Suite 1100
  Washington, DC 20004-1707
  Tel: 202-626-4000
  Email: ata@airlines.org
  http://www.airlines.org

For general information on aviation, contact
  Federal Aviation Administration
  800 Independence Avenue, SW, Room 810
  Washington, DC 20591
  Tel: 202-366-4000
  http://www.faa.gov

For information on union representation for baggage and cargo han-dlers, contact

**International Association of Machinists
and Aerospace Workers**
9000 Machinists Place
Upper Marlboro, MD 20772-2687
Tel: 301-967-4500
http://www.iamaw.org

Helicopter Pilots

OVERVIEW

Helicopter pilots serve in a wide range of fields from medicine to communications, and they are employed by both the government and private industry. They are vital in emergency situations, in gathering information, and in transporting people and cargo short distances. Helicopter pilots are employed across the United States and in other countries, and even in remote places throughout the world.

HISTORY

In the mid-1500s, the Italian inventor Leonardo da Vinci sketched a design of a flying vehicle that we now know as the helicopter. This design was impractical in full-sized form, and scientists and inventors experimented for the next three centuries to create a practical design for a flying vehicle. It was not until 1877 that Enrico Forlanini, an Italian professor, flew a steam-driven model helicopter for 20 seconds. Further experiments were attempted to increase flight time over the next few decades. With Orville and Wilbur Wright's groundbreaking flight of a fixed-wing aircraft on December 17, 1903, the modern age of aviation began. A Frenchmen named Louise Breguet constructed a helicopter that took a man aloft in 1907, but it was nearly three more decades before the first practical helicopter, the German Focke-Wulf 61, was produced in 1936. After World War II, great advances were made in the design and production of helicopters. They were used extensively in the Korean and Vietnam War to transport troops, supplies, and weapons. In the Vietnam War, helicopters were also heavily armed and used as gunships.

Today, helicopter pilots are counted on to perform a wide variety of tasks, including transporting sick and injured people to hospitals, reporting traffic conditions on radio and television news shows, and transporting workers and supplies to destinations that are inaccessible by other modes of transportation.

THE JOB

Helicopter pilots perform duties in medical evacuation, police and fire fighting work, forestry, construction, communications, agriculture, and offshore oil exploration. They may serve as air taxis, carry workers and supplies to oil rigs, rescue stranded flood victims, lift heavy materials to work sites, fly patients from one hospital to another, or give news and traffic updates for the media. Many, but not all, helicopter pilots who do police work are also law enforcement officers. Their work includes traffic regulation and survey, vehicle pursuits, surveillance, patrol, and search.

In addition to flying, helicopter pilots keep records of their aircraft's engine performance and file flight plans. Before and after flying they check the aircraft for problems and may even do repairs and general upkeep on the craft if they are licensed to do so.

While flying, helicopter pilots must monitor several dials and gauges to make sure the aircraft is functioning properly. They monitor changes in pressure, fuel, and temperature. Helicopter pilots also navigate using landmarks, compasses, maps, and radio equipment.

REQUIREMENTS

High School

All prospective pilots must complete high school. A college-preparatory curriculum is recommended because of the need for pilots to have at least some college education. Science and mathematics are two important subjects and you should also take advantage of any computer courses offered. You can start pursuing your pilot's license while in high school.

Postsecondary Training

Although helicopter pilots are not required to have a college degree, college credentials can lead to promotions and better jobs. Helicopter pilots may receive training in flying schools (which can be expensive) where they study the theory of flying, weather, radio, navigation, and Federal Aviation Administration (FAA) regulations. They also receive flight training.

Most of these pilots learn to fly as officers in the army. (For officers, a college degree is required.) To become licensed as a commercial helicopter pilot, a military pilot must pass the FAA military competency exam.

Certification or Licensing

To become a helicopter pilot, you must have a commercial pilot's license with a helicopter rating from the FAA. An applicant who is 18 years old and has 250 hours of flying time can apply for a commercial airplane pilot's license. In applying for this license, you must pass a rigid physical examination and a written test given by the FAA covering safe flight operations, federal aviation regulations, navigation principles, radio operation, and meteorology. You also must submit proof that the minimum flight-time requirements have been completed and, in a practical test, demonstrate flying skill and technical competence to a check pilot.

An instrument rating by the FAA and a restricted radio telephone operator's permit by the Federal Communications Commission are required.

Other Requirements

Good judgment, emotional balance, and the ability to think and act under pressure are ideal personal characteristics for working as a helicopter pilot. To qualify, pilots must be at least 21 years of age and meet the physical requirements of employers.

EXPLORING

If you are interested in flying, join the Explorers (Boy Scouts of America) or a high school aviation club. At 16 years of age, you can start taking flying lessons. One of the most valuable experiences for high school students who want to be a pilot is to learn to be a ham radio operator, which is one of the qualifications for commercial flying.

EMPLOYERS

Helicopter pilots work private companies and government agencies throughout the United States and the world. They can find work in the military and many industries including agriculture, fire fighting, police and public safety, mining, utilities, timber, broadcasting, and travel and tourism. Helicopter pilots also work for corporations, flight training schools, and for government agencies such as the FAA and the National Transportation Safety Board.

A helicopter pilot drops off a fire fighting crew near a forest fire. *(Bob Nichols, USDA)*

STARTING OUT

Most helicopter pilots receive their first job leads through the aviation schools where they received their training, federal and state employment agencies, private employment agencies, and job listings in the newspaper or on aviation-industry related websites.

ADVANCEMENT

Seniority, hours of flight time, and type of aircraft are the key factors in getting promotions in the helicopter industry. When starting out, most helicopter pilots fly the smaller single-engine aircraft. As they gain experience and hours of flying time, they may fly larger helicopters and obtain higher paying jobs. Pilots employed by large companies may be promoted to chief pilot or aviation department manager.

EARNINGS

The rate of pay for helicopter pilots is based on level of experience, the size and type of craft, responsibilities, region, and employer. According to *Rotor & Wing's* 2001 helicopter industry salary survey, chief pilots in the civil government earned salaries ranging from $37,000 to $140,000 a year. Commercial pilots and corporate pilots earned from $45,000 to $150,000. Salaries also vary by specialty. Flight training pilots earned an average of $45,000, EMS pilots earned $59,949, firefighting pilots earned $74,125, and offshore oil support pilots earned an average of $106,000 a year.

Most employers of helicopter pilots provide medical, dental, and life insurance as well as paid vacations of about three weeks. For performing special services, such as flying to remote areas, they receive bonuses.

WORK ENVIRONMENT

Some helicopter pilots work overtime, extra hours, and both daytime and night shifts. The number of hours helicopter pilots work depends on the type of employment. Air taxi pilots and police helicopter pilots may work 40 hours a week. Those who do police work may work more than 40 hours a week. Agricultural, forestry, and fire pilots may also work long hours.

Inside helicopters, pilots must remain seated in the cramped space for hours at a time. There is often mental stress involved in the constant alertness and concentration necessary for monitoring the craft's gauges and reading instruments. Fire fighting and law enforcement pilots are exposed to potential bodily harm while agricultural and construction pilots may be exposed to harsh chemicals.

OUTLOOK

The U.S. Department of Labor predicts that employment for aircraft pilots will grow about as fast as the average for all other occupations. There will be good opportunities in offshore oil support, emergency medical services, firefighting, and law enforcement. More jobs will be available in civil government and commercial transport than in corporate transport. Many employers are offering salary increases to keep qualified pilots.

FOR MORE INFORMATION

For information about industry publications, contact
  AHS International-The Vertical Flight Society
  217 North Washington Street
  Alexandria, VA 22314-2538
  Tel: 703-684-6777
  Email: Staff@vtol.org
  http://www.vtol.org

For information on licensing, contact
Federal Aviation Administration
800 Independence Ave, SW, Room 810
Washington, DC 20591
Tel: 202-366-4000
http://www.faa.gov

*For career information, educational opportunities, and to partici-
pate in online forums, visit the HSI website:*
Helicopter Association International (HSI)
1635 Prince Street
Alexandria VA 22314
Tel: 703-683-4646
http://www.rotor.com

Industrial Traffic Managers

QUICK FACTS

School Subjects
Business
Mathematics

Personal Skills
Communication/ideas
Leadership/management

Work Environment
Primarily indoors
Primarily one location

Minimum Education Level
High school diploma

Salary Range
$15,810 to $59,660 to
$100,000+

Certification or Licensing
Voluntary

Outlook
About as fast as the average

DOT
184

GOE
N/A

NOC
0713

O*NET-SOC
11-3071.01, 43-5071.00

OVERVIEW

Industrial traffic managers handle the booking, billing, claims, and related paperwork for the safe and efficient movement of cargo by air, water, truck, or rail. They analyze the costs of different forms of transport and calculate the shipping rates for the customers. There are approximately 111,000 transportation, storage, and distribution managers employed in the United States. Shipping, receiving, and traffic clerks hold about 803,000 jobs.

HISTORY

As the modes of transportation have improved over the centuries, so have the means of transporting freight from place to place. Businesses can now choose from among many alternatives—air, water, truck, or rail—to determine the best method for sending their goods. They want to find the method that will be the most efficient, economical, and reliable arrangement for each particular type of cargo. The job industrial traffic managers perform has helped add organization and efficiency to an increasingly complex process.

With the rise of mass production techniques in the 20th century, manufacturers have been able to produce more products than ever before. A company may produce hundreds of thousands of products each year, and each must reach its ultimate destination: the consumer. The vast numbers of products have created a need for people who specialize in seeing that these products are packed, shipped, and received properly and efficiently. Today's industrial traffic managers make

144

use of the latest technological innovations to coordinate the shipping and receiving of products worldwide.

THE JOB

Industrial traffic managers direct and coordinate workers who document, classify, route, and schedule outgoing freight and who verify and reship incoming freight at warehouses and other work sites. They also quote rates and give other information to customers and handle customer complaints about damaged, missing, or overcharged goods. Some traffic managers decide which method of transportation of goods is best. They investigate different means of transportation and then make their decisions based on the efficiency and cost. Computers have made the traffic manager's job much easier. In order to make important judgments, traffic managers must make distance and rate calculations that can be done easily and quickly with computers. Computer programs, with their ability to analyze cost-effectiveness, can also help traffic managers decide on the most efficient means of transporting goods.

Traffic agents contact industrial and commercial firms to solicit freight business. These workers call on prospective shippers to explain the advantages of using their company's services. They quote tariff rates, schedules, and operating conditions, such as loading or unloading practices. When an agreement is reached, the traffic agent may also serve as liaison between the shipper and the carrier, help settle complaints, or follow up on the handling of special goods, such as live animals, delicate equipment, or perishable goods. *Traffic clerks* keep records of incoming and outgoing freight by recording the destination, routing, weight, and tariffs. These workers may also be required to keep records of damaged freight and clients' claims of overcharge. *Shipping services sales representatives* perform similar work for parcel-delivery businesses.

Rate supervisors analyze rates and routes in an effort to find ways to reduce transportation costs. They supervise the work of *traffic-rate clerks*, who determine the rates that a transportation company will charge for shipping cargo of various kinds. *Freight rate analysts* also analyze rates, along with current and proposed government regulations, to determine how the transportation company should revise its rates and practices. These analysts also compile the shipping company's rate manual.

REQUIREMENTS

High School

Many jobs are available to high school graduates, especially with smaller companies, and part-time and summer employment is often available to high school students. You can prepare for a career as an industrial traffic manager by taking courses in economics, mathematics, science, and business administration.

Postsecondary Training

If you are interested in advancing to positions of greater responsibility, you are strongly advised to have at least some postsecondary education. More and more companies have begun to require one to two years of college education for entry into this field, especially when seeking employees interested in making a career with their company. Many community and junior colleges offer traffic and transportation curricula to prepare workers for employment as traffic agents and clerks. Some institutions combine course work with on-the-job experience in programs that lead to an associate's degree or a certificate of completion.

Certification and Licensing

The American Society of Transportation and Logistics offers the certified in transportation and logistics designation to applicants who pass exams in the following areas: general management principles and techniques, transportation economics and management, logistics systems management, public policy and legal issues in transportation and logistics, and international transport and logistics. Applicants must also satisfy a creative requirement by writing either a formal research paper or an academic thesis about a traffic-, transportation-, logistics-, or distribution management–related topic.

Other Requirements

Traffic agents and clerks implement the detailed transportation plans or programs that others have developed, as well as communicate these plans to others. To do this, you must be skilled in both verbal and written communication. You must be responsible, dependable, and exacting with details. You must also be able to work easily with numerical data. Basic computer skills are often required for tracking the flow of goods.

EXPLORING

The best opportunity for experience in this field would be a part-time or summer job as a clerk or truck helper with a transportation company or a local moving company. In these positions, you would be able to observe the work and responsibilities of traffic agents as well as talk with agents about their positions.

You may want to contact a college placement service or local or state employment services. In addition, work-experience programs offered by many companies enable you to become established with an employer while gaining valuable experience. You can also contact employers directly through letters of application. Check newspaper want ads for notices of job openings.

EMPLOYERS

Industrial traffic managers work for all kinds of companies that oversee the transportation of their goods and materials. Traffic agents work for companies that specialize in transportation.

STARTING OUT

Entry-level shipping and receiving positions generally do not require a high degree of educational achievement. Many positions are open to high school graduates, particularly in smaller companies. Management positions, however, are increasingly being filled by graduates of two-year college programs. Therefore, one of the best ways to find an entry-level position as an industrial traffic manager is to work with the job placement office of your community or technical college.

ADVANCEMENT

There are many paths for advancement in this field. For example, someone entering the field as a rate and claims clerk might eventually be promoted to a position as a rate analyst. A routing clerk could be promoted to terminal cargo manager, and a company representative could advance to the position of traffic manager. Industrial traffic managers who earn a bachelor's degree in logistics might be promoted to the position of logistics manager.

EARNINGS

Starting salaries depend greatly on the applicant's level of education, college experience, other relevant work experience, and the degree of responsibility of the position. According to the U.S. Department of Labor, transportation, storage, and distribution managers had median annual earnings of $59,660 in 2002. The lowest paid 10 percent earned less than $34,330 annually. The most experienced industrial traffic managers, often those with a master's degree in business, earn

$100,000 or more a year. Shipping, receiving, and traffic clerks earned salaries that ranged from less than $15,810 to more than $36,620 in 2002.

Fringe benefits vary widely, depending on the type and size of the company, although most will include vacations and holiday pay, health insurance plans, and in some cases, tuition-reimbursement plans.

WORK ENVIRONMENT

Because of the diverse characteristics of each particular mode of transportation, it is difficult to make a general statement about working conditions. Some positions consist of outdoor work, others are almost exclusively indoors, and some are combinations of the two. The hours may be long or shift work may be required since some terminals operate around the clock and certain cargoes must be dispatched as soon as they arrive. Some positions, however, require only regular hours with weekends off.

OUTLOOK

Large and medium-sized companies are increasingly using computers to store and retrieve records. Computerized conveyor systems, robotics, and trucks, as well as scanners are increasing productivity and eliminating the need for large numbers of workers. Traffic management can never be completely computerized, however. Managers will still be needed to arrange and oversee shipments before they go out and when they arrive. As a result, employment of industrial traffic managers is expected to grow about as fast as the average for all occupations through 2012, according to the U.S. Department of Labor. Traffic clerks will be more affected by automation as most firms attempt to save money by using computerized tracking systems. Employment for these workers will grow more slowly than the average through 2012.

FOR MORE INFORMATION

For information on certification, contact
American Society of Transportation and Logistics
1700 North Moore Street, Suite 1900
Arlington, VA 22209
Tel: 703-524-5011
Email: astl@nitl.org
http://www.astl.org

For information on college programs and to read the online publication Careers in Logistics, *visit the CLM website:*

Council of Logistics Management (CLM)
2805 Butterfield Road, Suite 200
Oak Brook, IL 60523-1170
Tel: 630-574-0985
Email: clmAdmin@clm1.org
http://www.clm1.org

Military Pilots

QUICK FACTS

School Subjects
Computer science
Government
Physics

Personal Skills
Leadership/management
Technical/scientific

Work Environment
Indoors and outdoors
Primarily multiple locations

Minimum Education Level
Bachelor's degree

Salary Range
$26,204 to $56,142 to
$142,499

Certification or Licensing
None available

Outlook
About as fast as the average

DOT
378, 632

GOE
N/A

NOC
2271

O*NET-SOC
55-1011.00, 55-2011.00,
55-3011.00, 55-3017.00

OVERVIEW

Military pilots fly various types of specialized aircraft to transport troops and equipment and to execute combat missions. Military aircraft make up of one of the world's largest fleets of specialized airplanes.

The U.S. armed forces are composed of five separate military services: the Army, Air Force, Marines, Navy, and Coast Guard (which is now part of the U.S. Department of Homeland Security). Pilots within these branches train, organize, and equip the nation's air services to support the national and international policies of the government.

Those who choose to join the armed forces dedicate their lives to protecting their fellow Americans. More than 2.5 million people served in the Armed Forces in 2003, and 1.4 million of these were on active duty. There are approximately 16,000 airplane pilots and 6,500 helicopter pilots in the military.

HISTORY

The air service grew from somewhat unusual beginnings. The Civil War marked the first use of aircraft in the U.S. military, when a balloon corps was attached to the Army of the Potomac. In 1892, a formal Balloon Corps was created as part of the army's Signal Corps. By 1907, a separate Aeronautical Division was created within the army. Air power proved invaluable a few years later during World War I, bringing about major changes in military strategy. As a result, the United States began to assert itself as an international military power, and accordingly, the Army Air Service was created as an independent unit in 1918, although it remained under army direction for a time.

With the surprise attack on Pearl Harbor in 1941, America was plunged into World War II. At the height of that war 13 million Americans fought in the different branches of the military services. When the war ended, the United States emerged as the strongest military power in the Western world. A large part of America's military success was due to the superiority of its air forces. Recognition of the strategic importance of air power led to the creation of the now wholly independent branch of service, the U.S. Air Force, in 1947. Two years later, the various branches of military service were unified under the Department of Defense.

Since then, military pilots have played an integral role during the Cold War, Korean War, the Vietnam War, the Persian Gulf War, and countless smaller skirmishes and engagements, as well as in non-combat and peacekeeping situations.

Reaction to the terrorist attacks of September 11, 2001, suddenly changed the role of the military from a peacekeeping force to an aggressor in the attempt to destroy the strongholds and training camps of terrorists around the world. President Bush said the war against terrorism would likely be a sustained effort over a long period of time. U.S. troops, warships, and dozens of fighter planes were deployed to south-central Asia and the Middle East and air and ground strikes began. In addition to military action, the administration planned to use diplomatic, law enforcement, and financial strategies against those believed responsible for the attacks.

THE JOB

Military pilots operate many different jet and propeller planes. Aircraft range from combat airplanes and helicopters, to supersonic fighters and bombers. In addition to actually flying aircraft, military pilots are also responsible for developing flight plans; checking weather reports; briefing and directing all crew members; and performing system operation checks to test the proper functioning of instrumentation, controls, and electronic and mechanical systems on the flight deck. They also are responsible for coordinating their takeoffs and landings with airplane dispatchers and air traffic controllers. At times, military pilots may be ordered to transport equipment and personnel, take reconnaissance photographs, spot and observe enemy positions, and patrol areas to carry out flight missions. After landing, military pilots must follow "afterlanding and shutdown" checklist procedures, and inform maintenance crews of any discrepancies or other problems noted during the flight. They must also present a written or oral flight report to their commanding officer.

Military aviation specialties include *flight navigators* or *radar technicians,* who use radio, radar, and other equipment to help military pilots determine aircraft position and determine its route of travel, and *flight instructors,* who teach flight students how to fly via classroom training and inflight instruction.

Opportunities as a military pilot are available in all five branches of the U.S. Armed Services. The following paragraphs detail these opportunities by military branch.

Although the Army is best known for its land-based occupations, it also employs military pilots to serve in combat, rescue, and reconnaissance settings. Army pilots are classified under the warrant officer designation along with other skilled experts in nonaviation fields.

The Air Force has the largest number of military pilots. These pilots work in a variety of specialty areas including bombers, airlifts, special operations, surveillance, and navigation. Specific job titles in this branch of the military include air battle managers, airlift pilots and navigators, bomber pilots and navigators, fighter pilots and navigators, reconnaissance/surveillance/electronic warfare pilots and navigators, special operations pilots and navigators, and tanker pilots and navigators.

Marine aviation officers provide air support for ground troops during battle. They also transport equipment and personnel to various destinations.

Pilots in the Navy are called *naval flight officers.* Unlike other military pilots, they take off and land their airplanes on both land bases and aircraft carriers. Depending on their specialty, they receive advanced training in air-to-air combat, bombing, search and rescue, aircraft carrier qualifications, over-water navigation, and low-level flying. Naval flight officer specialties include *turboprop maritime propeller pilots,* who track submarines, conduct surveillance, and gather photographic intelligence, and *Navy helicopter pilots,* who deliver supplies and personnel and participate in emergency search and rescue missions.

The U.S. Coast Guard is the only armed force in the United States with domestic law enforcement authority. Nearly 800 aviators at 26 air stations enforce federal laws and treaties and conduct military operations to safeguard the American homeland.

REQUIREMENTS

High School

You will need at least a high school degree in order to join the armed forces, and a college-preparatory curriculum is recommended. High school courses in science, mathematics, physics, computers, and physical education will be the most helpful. It's also a good idea to take a foreign language, which may expand your job opportunities. To enter the military, you must be at least 17 years old. Applicants who are age 17 must also have the consent of a parent or legal guardian.

Postsecondary Training

A four-year college degree is usually required to become a military pilot. Courses in engineering, meteorology, computer science, aviation law, business management, and military science are especially helpful. Physical education courses will also be important, as your physical health and endurance levels will constantly be challenged in the military.

There are several paths that you can choose from to get your post-secondary education. You may want to attend one of the four service academies: the U.S. Air Force Academy (for the Air Force), the U.S. Military Academy (for the Army), the U.S. Naval Academy (for the Navy and the Marines), or the U.S. Coast Guard Academy (for the Coast Guard). Competition to enter these institutions is intense. You will need to have a very strong academic background, involvement in community activities, and leadership experiences. Most applicants also need a nomination from an authorized source, which is usually a member of the U.S. Congress. If you choose one of these four academies, you will graduate with a bachelor's degree. You are then required to spend a minimum of five years on active duty, beginning as a junior officer.

Another option is to attend a four-year school that has a Reserve Officers Training Corps (ROTC) program. Most state-supported colleges and universities have aviation programs, as do many private schools. Some schools focus solely on aviation education, such as Embry-Riddle Aeronautical University and The University of North Dakota's Center for Aerospace Sciences.

Each branch of the Armed Services has specific training requirements for its military pilots. Training in all branches will include flight simulation, classroom training, and basic flight instruction. For more information on specific requirements, contact a recruiter for the branch in which you are interested in entering.

Certification or Licensing

The military does not offer certification or licensing for military pilots. During the advanced portion of your civilian flight training, though, you must pass the FAA's guidelines and regulations. If you hope to someday transfer your military skills to a similar job in the civilian sector (for example, with a commercial airline), you may need additional training and/or certification or licensing.

An F/A-18C Hornet pilot climbs
into the cockpit of his aircraft.
(U.S. Department of Defense)

Other Requirements

Stable physical and emotional health is essential for the aspiring pilot. Military pilots are expected to remain calm and levelheaded, no matter how stressful the situation. The physical requirements of this profession are very strict—you must have 20/20 vision with or without glasses, good hearing, normal heart rate and blood pressure, and no physical handicaps that could hinder performance.

You should have quick decision-making skills and reflexes to be a successful pilot. Decisiveness, self-confidence, good communication skills, and the ability to work well under pressure are also important personality traits. You should maintain an adaptable and flexible lifestyle, as your orders, missions, and station may change at any time.

Although military pilot careers are available to both men and women, some combat positions are only open to men.

EXPLORING

Military recruiters often visit high schools, so be sure to take advantage of this opportunity to learn more about this field. Take a tour of a military base or an aircraft carrier if you get the chance. Talk with family and friends who have served in the Armed Forces to get advice and information.

To get a real feel for what it's like to be a military pilot, check out one of several air combat schools that exist throughout the country. Through such programs, you can experience the cockpit of a fighter plane alongside an instructor, and even experience "dogfighting" in the sky. Air Combat USA, which is one such program, operates out of 15 airports nationwide. See the the end of this article to learn more.

EMPLOYERS

Military pilots are employed by the U.S. government. More than 2.5 million people served in the armed forces in 2003. There are approximately 16,000 airplane pilots and 6,500 helicopter pilots in the military.

STARTING OUT

Once you've decided to become a military pilot, you should contact a military recruiter. The recruiter will help answer questions and suggest different options. To start out in any branch of the military, you must pass medical and physical tests, the Armed Services Vocational Aptitude Battery exam, and basic training. You must also sign an enlistment contract. This is a legal agreement that will bind you to a certain amount of military service, usually eight years. Active duty comprises two to six years of this agreement, and the remainder is normally spent in the reserves.

ADVANCEMENT

Each military branch has 10 officers' grades (O-1 through O-10). The higher the number is, the more advanced a person's rank is. The various branches of the military have somewhat different criteria for promoting individuals; in general, however, promotions depend on factors such as length of time served, demonstrated abilities, recommendations, and scores on written exams. Promotions become more and more competitive as people advance in rank.

Military pilots may train for different aircraft and missions. Eventually, they may advance to senior officer or command positions. Military pilots with superior skills and training may advance to the position of *astronaut*. Astronauts pilot the space shuttle on scientific and defense-related missions.

EARNINGS

Congress sets the pay scales for the military after hearing recommendations from the president. The pay for equivalent grades is the same in all services (that is, anyone with a grade of 0-4, for example, will have the same basic pay whether in the Army, Navy, Marines, Air Force, or Coast Guard). In addition to basic pay, personnel who frequently and regularly participate in combat may earn hazardous duty pay. Other special allowances include special duty pay and foreign duty pay. Earnings start relatively low but increase on a fairly regular basis as individuals advance in rank. When reviewing earnings, it is important to keep in mind that members of the military receive free housing, food, and health care—items that civilians typically pay for themselves.

All military pilots serve as officers in their respective branches. According to the Defense Finance and Accounting Service, officers starting out at a grade of O-1 received basic monthly pay of $2,183.70 in 2003. This would make for an annual salary of approximately $26,204. An officer with the grade O-5 and more than four years of experience earned $4,678.50 per month, or approximately $56,142 per year. And an officer with the top grade of O-10 and more than 20 years of experience had monthly basic earnings of $11,874.90, or approximately $142,499 annually.

Additional benefits for military workers include uniform allowances, 30 days of paid vacation time per year, and the opportunity to retire after 20 years of service. Generally, those retiring will receive 40 percent of the average of the highest three years of their base pay. This amount rises incrementally, reaching 75 percent of the average of the highest three years of base pay after 30 years of service. All retirement provisions are subject to change, however, and you should verify them as well as current salary information before you enlist. Military pilots who retire after 20 years of service are usually in their 40s and thus have plenty of time, as well as an accumulation of skills, with which to start a second career as a civilian pilot or in a related field.

WORK ENVIRONMENT

The work environment for military pilots is rewarding, varied, and sometimes stressful. Pilots may be assigned to one or more air bases around the world. They may take off and land on aircraft carriers, at conventional airports, in desert conditions under fierce fire from the enemy, or in countless other settings. They may fly the same routes for extended periods of time, but no two flights are ever the same. Military pilots can expect excitement and the chance to see the world, but they are responsible for the safety and protection of others.

OUTLOOK

The outlook for military workers, including military pilots, is expected to be good through 2012, according to the U.S. Department of Labor. Approximately 365,000 new enlistees and officers must join annually to fill vacated spots. In recent years some branches, such as the Navy, have fallen short of meeting their recruitment goals, and opportunities in these branches are even more plentiful than the average. While political and economic conditions will have an influence on the military's duties and employment outlook, it is a fact that the country will always need military pilots, both for defense and to protect its interests and citizens around the world.

FOR MORE INFORMATION

To learn more about combat school experience, as well as pilot proficiency training, visit
Air Combat USA
http://www.aircombatusa.com

For a RealAudio and RealVideo experience of aviation, as well as information on aviation safety, becoming a pilot, and other information, contact
CyberAir Airpark
http://www.cyberair.com

Read up on military news and developments by visiting
Defense-Aerospace.com
http://www.defense-aerospace.com

To get information on specific branches of the military, check out this site, which is the home of ArmyTimes.com, NavyTimes.com, AirForceTimes.com, and MarineCorpsTimes.com:
Military City
http://www.militarycity.com

If you're thinking of joining the Armed Forces, take a look at the following site, which guides students and parents through the decision:
Today's Military
http://www.todaysmilitary.com

For information on becoming a military pilot, contact
United States Air Force
http://www.airforce.com/index_fr.htm

United States Army
http://www.goarmy.com/job/warrant

United States Marine Corps
http://www.marines.com/officer_programs

United States Navy
http://www.navy.com/officer/aviation

United States Coast Guard Recruiting
http://www.gocoastguard.com/officerindex.html

Pilots

OVERVIEW

Pilots perform many different kinds of flying jobs. In general, pilots operate an aircraft for the transportation of passengers, freight, mail, or for other commercial purposes. There are approximately 100,000 civilian aircraft pilots and flight engineers employed in the United States.

HISTORY

The age of modern aviation is generally considered to have begun with the famous flight of Orville and Wilbur Wright's heavier-than-air machine on December 17, 1903. On that day, the Wright brothers flew their machine four times and became the first airplane pilots. In the early days of aviation, the pilot's job was quite different from that of the pilot of today. As he flew the first plane, for instance, Orville Wright was lying on his stomach in the middle of the bottom wing of the plane. There was a strap across his hips, and to turn the plane, Wright had to tilt his hips from side to side.

Aviation developed rapidly as designers raced to improve upon the Wright brothers' design. During the early years of flight, many aviators earned a living as "barnstormers," entertaining people with stunts and by taking passengers on short flights around the countryside. Airplanes were quickly adapted to military use. Pilots soon became famous for their war exploits and for feats of daring and endurance as improvements in airplane designs allowed them to make transcontinental, transoceanic, or transpolar flights. As airplanes grew more complex and an entire industry developed, pilots were joined by copilots and flight engineers to assist in operating the plane.

QUICK FACTS

School Subjects
Mathematics
Physics

Personal Skills
Leadership/management
Technical/scientific

Work Environment
Primarily indoors
Primarily multiple locations

Minimum Education Level
Some postsecondary training

Salary Range
$55,800 to $109,580 to $145,000+

Certification or Licensing
Required by all states

Outlook
About as fast as the average

DOT
196

GOE
05.04.01

NOC
2271

O*NET-SOC
53-2011.00, 53-2012.00

The airline industry originated from the United States government-run air mail service. Pilots who flew for this service were praised in newspapers, and their work in this new advanced industry made their jobs seem glamorous. But during the Great Depression, pilots faced the threat of losing their high pay and status. The Air Line Pilots Association stepped in and won federal protection for the airline pilot's job. In 1978, when the airline industry was deregulated, many expected the pay and status of pilots to decrease. However, the steady growth of airlines built a demand for good pilots and their value remained high.

Today, pilots perform a variety of services. Many pilots fly for the military services. Pilots with commercial airlines fly millions of passenger and cargo flights each year. Other pilots use airplanes for crop-dusting, pipeline inspection, skydiving, and advertising. Many pilots provide instruction for flight schools. A great many pilots fly solely for pleasure, and many people own their own small planes.

THE JOB

The best known pilots are the commercial pilots who fly for the airlines. Responsible, skilled professionals, they are among the highest paid workers in the country. The typical pilot flight deck crew includes the *captain,* who is the pilot in command, and the *copilot,* or *first officer.* In larger aircraft, there may be a third member of the crew, called the *flight engineer,* or *second officer.* The captain of a flight is in complete command of the crew, the aircraft, and the passengers or cargo while they are in flight. In the air, the captain also has the force of law. The aircraft may hold 30 people or 300 or be completely loaded with freight, depending on the airline and type of operations. The plane may be fitted with either turbojet, turboprop (which are propellers driven by jet engines), or reciprocating propeller engines. An aircraft may operate near the speed of sound and at altitudes as high as 40,000 feet.

In addition to actually flying the aircraft, pilots must perform a variety of safety-related tasks. Before each flight, they must determine weather and flight conditions, ensure that sufficient fuel is on board to complete the flight safely, and verify the maintenance status of the aircraft. The captain briefs all crew members, including the flight attendants, about the flight. Pilots must also perform system operation checks to test the proper functioning of instrumentation, controls, and electronic and mechanical systems on the flight deck. Pilots coordinate their flight plan with airplane dispatchers and air traffic controllers. Flight plans include information about the airplane, the passenger or cargo load, and the air route the pilot is expected to take.

Once all preflight duties have been performed, the captain taxis the aircraft to the designated runway and prepares for takeoff. Takeoff speeds must be calculated based on the aircraft's weight. The aircraft systems, levers, and switches must be in proper position for takeoff. After takeoff, the pilots may engage an electrical device known as the autopilot. This device can be programmed to maintain the desired course and altitude. With or without the aid of the autopilot, pilots must constantly monitor the aircraft's systems.

Because pilots may encounter turbulence, emergencies, and other hazardous situations during a flight, good judgment and quick response are extremely important. Pilots receive periodic training and evaluation on their handling of in-flight abnormalities and emergencies and on their operation of the aircraft during challenging weather conditions. As a further safety measure, airline pilots are expected to adhere to checklist procedures in all areas of flight operations.

During a flight, pilots monitor aircraft systems, keep a watchful eye on local weather conditions, review checklists, and maintain constant communication with the air traffic controllers along the flight route. The busiest times for pilots are during takeoff and landing. The weather conditions at the aircraft's destination must be obtained and analyzed. The aircraft must be maneuvered and properly configured to make a landing on the runway. When the cloud cover is low and visibility is poor, pilots rely solely on the instruments on the flight deck. These instruments include an altimeter and an artificial horizon. Pilots select the appropriate radio navigation frequencies and corresponding course for the ground-based radio and microwave signals that provide horizontal, and in some cases vertical, guidance to the landing runway.

After the pilots have safely landed the aircraft, the captain taxis it to the ramp or gate area where passengers and cargo are off-loaded. Pilots then follow "afterlanding and shutdown" checklist procedures, and inform maintenance crews of any discrepancies or other problems noted during the flight.

Pilots must also keep detailed logs of their flight hours, both for payroll purposes and to comply with Federal Aviation Administration (FAA) regulations. Pilots with major airlines generally have few nonflying duties. Pilots with smaller airlines, charter services, and other air service companies may be responsible for loading the aircraft, refueling, keeping records, performing minor repairs and maintenance, and arranging for major repairs.

A pilot, copilot, and flight engineer prepare for takeoff.
(American Airlines)

The *chief pilot* directs the operation of the airline's flight department. This individual is in charge of training new pilots, preparing schedules and assigning flight personnel, reviewing their performance, and improving their morale and efficiency. Chief pilots make sure that all legal and government regulations affecting flight operations are observed, advise the airline during contract negotiations with the pilots' union, and handle a multitude of administrative details.

In addition to airline pilots, there are various other types of pilots. *Business pilots,* or *executive pilots,* fly for businesses that have their own planes. These pilots transport cargo, products, or people and maintain the company's planes as well. *Test pilots,* though there are not many, are very important. Combining knowledge of flying with an engineering background, they test new models of planes and make sure they function properly. *Flight instructors* are pilots who teach others how to fly. They teach in classrooms or provide inflight instruction. Other pilots work as *examiners,* or *check pilots.* They fly with experienced pilots as part of their periodic review; they may also give examinations to pilots applying for licenses.

Some pilots are employed in specialties, such as *photogrammetry pilots,* who fly planes or helicopters over designated areas and photograph the earth's surface for mapping and other purposes.

Facilities-flight-check pilots fly specially equipped planes to test air navigational aids, air traffic controls, and communications equipment and to evaluate installation sites for such equipment.

REQUIREMENTS

High School

All prospective pilots must complete high school. A college-preparatory curriculum is recommended because of the need for pilots to have at least some college education. Science and mathematics are two important subjects and you should also take advantage of any computer courses offered. You can start pursuing your pilot's license while in high school.

Postsecondary Training

Most companies that employ pilots require at least two years of college training; many require applicants to be college graduates. Courses in engineering, meteorology, physics, and mathematics are helpful in preparing for a pilot's career. Flying is taught in military and civilian flying schools. There are approximately 600 civilian flying schools certified by the FAA, including some colleges and universities that offer degree credit for pilot training. Pilots leaving the military are in great demand.

Certification or Licensing

To become a pilot, certain rigid training requirements must be met. Although obtaining a private pilot's license is not difficult, it may be quite difficult to obtain a commercial license. If you are 16 or over and can pass the rigid mandatory physical examination, you may apply for permission to take flying instruction. This instruction consists of classroom education and flight training from an FAA-certified flight instructor.

Before you make your first solo flight, you must get a medical certificate (certifying that you are in good health) and an instructor-endorsed student pilot certificate. In order to get the student pilot certificate, you must pass a test given by the flight instructor. This test will have questions about FAA rules as well as questions about the model and make of the aircraft you will fly. If you pass the test and the instructor feels you are prepared to make a solo flight, the instructor will sign (endorse) your pilot certificate and logbook.

To apply for a private pilot's license, you must take a written examination. To qualify for it, you must be at least 17 years of age,

Types of Pilot Licenses

Student pilot certificate (license): Used for the initial training period of flying. Student pilots must fly with a flight instructor and can only fly solo after receiving appropriate endorsements from their flight instructor.

Recreational pilot certificate: Limits the pilot to specific classes and categories of aircraft, a limited number of passengers, the distance that may be flown from the point of departure, and flight into controlled airports.

Private pilot certificate: Allows a pilot to carry passengers and use his or her aircraft for limited business purposes.

Commercial pilot certificate: Allows a pilot to fly for compensation and hire.

Airline transport pilot certificate: Required to fly as captain by some air transport operations.

Source: Federal Aviation Administration

successfully fulfill a solo flying requirement of 20 hours or more, and meet instrument flying and cross-country flying requirements.

All pilots and copilots must be licensed by the FAA before they can do any type of commercial flying. An applicant who is 18 years old and has 250 hours of flying time can apply for a commercial airplane pilot's license. In applying for this license, you must pass a rigid physical examination and a written test given by the FAA covering safe flight operations, federal aviation regulations, navigation principles, radio operation, and meteorology. You also must submit proof that the minimum flight-time requirements have been completed and, in a practical test, demonstrate flying skill and technical competence to a check pilot. Before you receive an FAA license, you must also receive a rating for the kind of plane you can fly (single-engine, multi-engine, or seaplane) and for the specific type of plane, such as Boeing 707 or 747.

An instrument rating by the FAA and a restricted radio telephone operator's permit by the Federal Communications Commission are required. All airline captains must have an air transport pilot license. Applicants for this license must be at least 23 years old and have a minimum of 1,500 hours of flight time, including night flying and instrument time. All pilots are subject to two-year flight reviews, regular six-month FAA flight checks, simulator tests, and medical exams. The FAA also makes unannounced spot-check inspections of all pilots.

Jet pilots, helicopter pilots, and agricultural pilots all have special training in their respective fields.

Other Requirements
Sound physical and emotional health are essential requirements for aspiring pilots. Emotional stability is necessary because the safety of other people depends upon a pilot remaining calm and levelheaded, no matter how trying the situation. Physical health is equally important. You must have 20/20 vision with or without glasses, good hearing; normal heart rate and blood pressure, and no physical handicaps that could hinder performance.

EXPLORING

High school students who are interested in flying may join the Explorers (Boy Scouts of America) or a high school aviation club. At 16 years of age, you may start taking flying lessons. One of the most valuable experiences for high school students who want to be a pilot is to learn to be a ham radio operator, which is one of the qualifications for commercial flying.

EMPLOYERS

There are approximately 100,000 commercial pilots in the United States. The commercial airlines, including both passenger and cargo transport companies, are the primary employers of pilots. Pilots also work in general aviation, and many are trained and employed by the military.

STARTING OUT

A large percentage of commercial pilots have received their training in the armed forces. A military pilot who wants to apply for a commercial airplane pilot's license is required to pass the Federal Aviation Regulations examination if application is made within a year after leaving the service.

Pilots possessing the necessary qualifications and license may apply directly to a commercial airline for a job. If accepted, they will go through a company orientation course, usually including both classroom instruction and practical training in company planes.

Those who are interested in becoming business pilots will do well to start their careers in mechanics. They may also have military flying experience, but the strongest recommendation for a business pilot's job is an airframe and powerplant (A and P) rating. They should also have at least 500 hours of flying time and have both commercial and instrument ratings on their license. They apply directly to the firm for which they would like to work.

ADVANCEMENT

Many beginning pilots start out as copilots. Seniority is the pilot's most important career asset. If pilots leave one employer and go to another, they must start from the bottom again, no matter how much experience was gained with the first employer. The position of captain on a large airline is a high-seniority, high-prestige, and high-paying job. Pilots may also advance to the position of check pilot, testing other pilots for advanced ratings; chief pilot, supervising the work of other pilots; or to administrative or executive positions with a commercial airline (ground operations). They may also become self-employed, opening a flying business, such as a flight instruction, agricultural aviation, air-taxi, or charter service.

EARNINGS

Airline pilots are among the highest paid workers in the country. Salaries vary widely depending on a number of factors, including the specific airline, type of aircraft flown, number of years with a company, and level of experience. Airline pilots are also paid more for international and nighttime flights.

The U.S. Department of Labor reports that median annual earnings of airline pilots, copilots, and flight engineers were $109,580 in 2002. The lowest 10 percent earned less than $55,800 and more than 25 percent earned more than $145,000. Commercial pilots had median annual earnings of $47,970 in 2002. Salaries ranged from less than $26,100 to more than $101,460.

Pilots with commercial airlines receive life and health insurance and retirement benefits; if they fail their FAA physical exam during their career, they are eligible to receive disability benefits. Some airlines give pilots allowances for buying and cleaning their uniforms. Pilots and their families may usually fly free or at reduced fares on their own or other airlines.

WORK ENVIRONMENT

Airline pilots work with the best possible equipment and under highly favorable circumstances. They command a great deal of respect.

Although many pilots regularly fly the same routes, no two flights are ever the same. FAA regulations limit airline pilots to no more than 100 flying hours per month. Most airline pilots fly approximately 75 hours per month and spend another 75 hours a month on nonflying duties.

While being an airline pilot can be a rewarding career, it can also be extremely stressful. During flights, they must concentrate on many items. They must always be alert to changes in conditions and to any problems that may occur. They are often responsible for hundreds of lives besides their own, and they are always aware that flying contains an element of risk. During emergencies, they must react quickly, logically, and decisively. Pilots often work irregular hours, may be away from home a lot, and are subject to jet lag and other conditions associated with flying. Pilots employed with smaller airlines may also be required to perform other, nonflying duties, which increase the number of hours they work each month.

For other pilots who handle small planes, emergency equipment, and supply delivery or routes to remote and isolated areas, the hazards may be more evident. Dropping medical supplies in Central Africa, flying relief supplies into war zones, or delivering mail to northern Alaska are more difficult tasks than most pilots face. Business pilot schedules may be highly irregular and they must be on call for a great portion of their off-duty time. Business pilots and most private and small plane pilots are also frequently called upon to perform maintenance and repairs.

Today, even commercial pilots face dangers that rival those encountered by small-plane pilots in war-torn or hard-to-reach areas. Airplanes have been a favorite target for terrorist activity for a number of years because they provide easy access to large numbers of hostages and transportation anywhere in the world. In recent years, all kinds of safety and security measures have been implemented at airports and on board aircraft. Engineers are designing ways to secure cockpits to protect pilots and crew, as well as ways to communicate dangers to ground crew. Even so, flying an aircraft carries risks that are on the minds of all pilots today.

OUTLOOK

The U.S. Department of Labor predicts that employment for pilots will grow about as fast as the average for all occupations through 2012. The entire airline industry has slowed. More than 100,000 airline employees were laid off after the 2001 terrorist attacks. To keep from going bankrupt, many airlines will undergo restructuring that will involve more layoffs and hiring freezes.

The airline industry expects a slow recovery process. It will take some time for crew and passengers to become accustomed to heightened security procedures and for traveler confidence to return. To compound problems, the airline industry is extremely sensitive to changes in the economy. When the economy suffers a downturn, everyone is less likely to spend money on air travel.

Opportunities will be best at regional airlines and low-fare carriers, which have experienced faster growth than the major airlines. Pilots who fly for air cargo carriers will also have good opportunities as these companies receive more shipping business as a result of security restrictions on the shipping of freight via passenger airlines. Employment for flight engineers is expected to decline as more planes are built that require only two-person crews.

FOR MORE INFORMATION

To read Looking for a Career Where the Sky Is The Limit?, *visit the ALPA website.*

Air Line Pilots Association
535 Herndon Parkway
Herndon, VA 20170
Tel: 703-689-2270
http://www.alpa.org

To read The Airline Handbook, *visit the ATAA website.*

Air Transport Association of
    America
1301 Pennsylvania Avenue, NW, Suite 1100
Washington, DC 20004-1707
Tel: 202-626-4000
Email: ata@airlines.org
http://www.airlines.org

For information on licensing, contact
Federal Aviation Administration
800 Independence Avenue, SW
Room 810
Washington, DC 20591
Tel: 202-366-4000
http://www.faa.gov

For career information, contact
Aviation Information Resources Inc.
1001 Riverdale Court
Atlanta, GA 30337
Tel: 800-217-2777
http://www.jet-jobs.com

For a RealAudio and RealVideo experience of aviation, as well as information on aviation safety, becoming a pilot, and other information, contact
CyberAir Airpark
http://www.cyberair.com

INTERVIEW

Dave Smith has been an airline pilot for seven years. He spoke with the editors of Careers in Focus: Aviation *about his career.*

Q. What are your primary and secondary job duties.

A. My primary job duties include:
- flying my assigned trip schedule, with the safety of passengers, crew, and equipment being of the utmost importance
- promoting on-time performance as much as possible
- helping to train and develop first officers I fly with, making sure they fly according to procedure
- following security procedures
- supervising and counseling other crew members

My secondary job duties include:
- ensuring passenger comfort and service
- keeping current on updated procedures and keeping pilot manuals current
- performing a simulator proficiency check every six months
- renewing my pilot's medical certificate every six months with a doctor's exam
- promoting my company's image in a positive manner

Q. How did you train for this job? What was your college major?

A. I trained for this job by attending a flight school at a university. I majored in aviation management. I completed the school's professional pilot program, earning all of my flight ratings there, including my flight instructor certificate. I then became a flight instructor in order to build the flight hours and experience needed to be hired by a regional airline. After about a year and a half of flight instructing, I had the 1,200 flight hours required to be hired by my employer.

Q. How/where did you get your first job in this field? What did you do?

A. I got my first job in this field as a flight instructor at the university where I learned to fly. I was a student instructor with two students assigned to me. I was able to get enough experience from student teaching to get my next job as a full-time flight instructor in Brownsville, Texas, where I received most of my flight experience.

Q. What are the most important personal and professional qualities for pilots?

A. Some of the most important personal and professional qualities of pilots are:
- reliability
- an ability to interact and cooperate with others
- strong problem-solving abilities
- an ability to work under stressful situations
- moderate math skills
- good spatial orientation (ability to read maps, visualize the aircraft in reference to the ground, etc.)
- some manual dexterity (for the actual flying of the aircraft)

Q. What are some of the pros and cons of your job?

A. Some of the pros of my job are:
- travel to many different destinations
- good flight benefits which allow very cheap/free air travel
- potential for high salary
- respect from the public
- good retirement benefits if you work for a major airline
- flying aircraft can be enjoyable while also giving a sense of accomplishment

Some of the cons of my job are:
- Pilots are away from home for long periods of time.
- Limited choices of where to be based, which prompts many people to commute to work from other cities. This requires flying to work and even more time away from home.
- The airline industry can be very volatile and cyclical—at least in some years.

- Pilots are subject to constant scrutiny from the Federal Aviation Administration, their airline, and the public.
- A large financial burden is required in trying to get to land a high-paying airline job. Pilots must take underpaying jobs in order to get to the larger airlines. Flight training is also expensive and can result in huge college loans.
- You are out of a job if your airline folds, and if you go to another airline you must start at the bottom of the seniority list, meaning your pay scale starts over at the bottom.
- Flight schedules can be physically draining with long work hours and short rest periods.

Q. What advice do you have to offer students as they graduate and look for jobs as pilots?

A. The most important piece of advice I have for students interested in becoming a pilot is to be patient and persistent. It is not always easy finding the job you want, but sometimes you have to just go to different airports and talk to people and hand out your resume. Networking is the best way to find jobs in aviation, so if your friends get hired, they can often help you get hired as well.

Airline hiring is cyclical, so you sometimes have to wait until conditions are right for jobs to open up, but eventually they will, so you can't give up. Once major airlines start hiring, they will hire commuter pilots who then must be replaced by flight instructors or cargo pilots who must be replaced by flight students, and then the whole industry is suddenly hiring at once.

Q. What is the future employment outlook for pilots?

A. It's unclear right now since 9/11, but it seems to be tied to the economy. When the economy is good the airlines do well, but when the economy is bad the airlines suffer. Since 9/11, things have not been good at most airlines and there have been many furloughs. Currently, the economy has been getting a little better and there seems to be a lot more optimism at the airlines, with rumors of pilot recalls and pilot hiring. In the end, though, the most important factor will be keeping flights safe from terrorism. Further terror attacks on aircraft would be devastating to the industry, and so ensuring security is of utmost concern.

Reservation and Ticket Agents

OVERVIEW

Reservation and ticket agents are employed by airlines, bus companies, railroads, and cruise lines to help customers in several ways. *Reservation agents* make and confirm travel arrangements for passengers by using computers and manuals to determine timetables, taxes, and other information.

Ticket agents sell tickets in terminals or in separate offices. Like reservation agents, they also use computers and manuals containing scheduling, boarding, and rate information to plan routes and calculate ticket costs. They determine whether seating is available, answer customer inquiries, check baggage, and direct passengers to proper places for boarding. They may also announce arrivals and departures and assist passengers in boarding. There are approximately 177,000 reservation and ticket agents employed in the United States. Approximately 60 percent are employed by airlines.

HISTORY

Since the earliest days of commercial passenger transportation (by boat or stagecoach), someone has been responsible for making sure that space is available and that everyone on board pays the proper fare. As transportation grew into a major industry over the years, the job of making reservations and selling tickets became a specialized occupation.

The airline industry experienced its first boom in the early 1930s. By the end of that decade, millions of people were flying each year. Since the introduction of passenger-carrying jet planes in 1958, the number of people traveling by air has multiplied many times over. The majority of reservation and ticket agents now work for airlines.

A number of innovations have helped make the work of reservation and ticket agents easier and more efficient. The introduction of automated telephone services allows customers to check on flight availability and arrival/departure times without having to wait to speak to an agent. Computers have both simplified the agents' work and put more resources within their reach. Since the 1950s, many airlines have operated computerized scheduling and reservation systems, either individually or in partnership with other airlines. Until recently, these systems were not available to the general consumer. In the last decade, however, the growth of the Internet has permitted travelers to access scheduling and rate information, make reservations, and purchase tickets without contacting an agent. Airlines now offer electronic tickets, which they expect will eventually replace the traditional paper ticket. Despite these innovations, there will always be a need for reservation and ticketing agents, primarily for safety and security purposes. These employees still fill a vital role in the transportation industry.

THE JOB

Airline reservation agents are sales agents who work in large central offices run by airline companies. Their primary job is to book and confirm reservations for passengers on scheduled flights. At the request of the customer or a ticket agent, they plan the itinerary and other travel arrangements. While many agents still use timetables, airline manuals, reference guides, and tariff books, most of this work is performed using specialized computer programs.

Computers are used to make, confirm, change, and cancel reservations. After asking for the passenger's destination, desired travel time, and airport of departure, reservation agents type the information into a computer and quickly obtain information on all flight schedules and seating availability. If the plane is full, the agent may suggest an alternative flight or check to see space is available on another airline that flies to the same destination. Agents may even book seats on competing airlines, especially if their own airline can provide service on the return trip.

Reservation agents answer telephone inquiries about such things as schedules, fares, arrival and departure times, and cities serviced by their airline. They may maintain an inventory of passenger space available so they can notify other personnel and ticket stations of changes and try to book all flights to capacity. Some reservation agents work in more specialized areas, handling calls from travel agents or booking flights for members of frequent flyer programs. Agents working with international airlines must also be informed of visa regulations and other travel developments. This information is usually supplied by the *senior reservation agent,* who supervises and coordinates the activities of the other agents.

General transportation ticket agents for any mode of travel (air, bus, rail, or ship) sell tickets to customers at terminals or at separate ticket offices. Like reservation agents, they book space for customers. In addition, they use computers to prepare and print tickets, calculate fares, and collect payment. At the terminals they check and tag luggage, direct passengers to the proper areas for boarding, keep records of passengers on each departure, and help with customer problems, such as lost baggage or missed connections. Airline ticket agents may have additional duties, such as paging arriving and departing passengers and finding accommodations or new travel arrangements for passengers in the event of flight cancellations.

In airports, *gate agents* assign seats, issue boarding passes, make public address announcements of departures and arrivals, and help elderly or disabled passengers board the planes. In addition, they may also provide information to disembarking passengers about ground transportation, connecting flights, and local hotels.

Regardless of where they work, reservation and transportation ticket agents must be knowledgeable about their companies' policies and procedures, as well as the standard procedures of their industry. They must be aware of the availability of special promotions and services and be able to answer any questions customers may have.

REQUIREMENTS

High School

Reservation and ticket agents are generally required to have at least a high school diploma. Applicants should be able to type and must have good communication and problem-solving skills. Because computers are being used more and more in this field, you should have a basic knowledge of computers and computer software. Previous experience working with the public is also helpful for the job. Knowledge of geography and foreign languages are other valuable skills, especially for international service agents.

Postsecondary Training

Some college is preferred, although it is not considered essential for the job. Some colleges now offer courses specifically focused on ticket reservations.

Reservation agents are given about a month of classroom instruction. Here you will be taught how to read schedules, calculate fares, and plan itineraries. They learn how to use computer programs to get information and reserve space efficiently. They also study company policies and government regulations that apply to the industry.

Transportation ticket agents receive less training, consisting of about one week of classroom instruction. They learn how to read tickets and schedules, assign seats, and tag baggage. This is followed by one week of on-the-job training, working alongside an experienced agent. After mastering the simpler tasks, the new ticket agents are trained to reserve space, make out tickets, and handle the boarding gate.

Other Requirements

Because you will be in constant contact with the public, professional appearance, a clear and pleasant speaking voice, and a friendly personality are important qualities. You need to be tactful in keeping telephone time to a minimum without alienating your customers. In addition, you should enjoy working with people, have a good memory, and be able to maintain your composure when working with harried or unhappy travelers. Agents form a large part of the public image of their company.

Although not a requirement, many agents belong to labor unions, such as the Transport Workers Union of America and the International Brotherhood of Teamsters.

EXPLORING

You may wish to apply for part-time or summer work with transportation companies in their central offices or at terminals. A school counselor can help you arrange an information interview with an experienced reservation and transportation ticket agent. Talking to an agent directly about his or her duties can help you to become more familiar with transportation operations.

EMPLOYERS

Reservation and ticket agents hold approximately 177,000 jobs in the United States. Commercial airlines are the main employers. However,

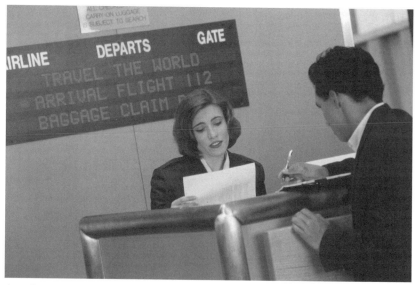

A ticket agent checks in a passenger. *(Photo Disc)*

other transportation companies, such as rail, ship, and bus lines, also require their services.

STARTING OUT

To find part-time or summer work, apply directly to the personnel or employment offices of transportation companies. Ask your school counselor or college placement director for information about job openings, requirements, and possible training programs. Additionally, contact transportation unions for lists of job openings.

ADVANCEMENT

With experience and a good work record, some reservation and ticket agents can be promoted to supervisory positions. They can also become city and district sales managers for ticket offices. Beyond this, opportunities for advancement are limited. However, achieving seniority within a company can give an agent the first choice of shifts and available overtime.

EARNINGS

According to the U.S. Department of Labor, reservation and transportation ticket agents earned median salaries of $25,350 in 2002.

The lowest paid 10 percent of these workers made less than $17,010 per year, while the highest paid 10 percent earned more than $44,910 annually.

Most agents can earn overtime pay; many employers also pay extra for night work. Benefits vary according to the place of work, experience, and union membership; however, most receive vacation and sick pay, health insurance, and retirement plans. Agents, especially those employed by the airlines, often receive free or reduced-fare transportation for themselves and their families.

WORK ENVIRONMENT

Reservation and ticket agents generally work 40 hours per week. Those working in reservations typically work in cubicles with their own computer terminals and telephone headsets. They are often on the telephone and at their computers all day long. Conversations with customers and computer activity may be monitored and recorded by their supervisors for evaluation and quality reasons. Agents might also be required to achieve sales or reservations quotas. During holidays or when special promotions and discounts are being offered, agents are especially busy. At these times or during periods of severe weather, passengers may become difficult. Handling customer frustrations can be stressful, but agents must maintain composure and a pleasant manner when speaking with customers.

Ticket agents working in airports face a busy and noisy environment. They may stand most of the day and lift heavy objects such as luggage and packages. During holidays and busy times, their work can become extremely hectic as they process long lines of waiting customers. Storms and other factors may delay or even cancel flights. Like reservation agents, ticket agents may be confronted with upset passengers, but must be able to maintain composure at all times.

OUTLOOK

According to the U.S. Department of Labor, employment for reservation and ticket agents is expected to grow about as fast as the average for all occupations through 2012. Technology is changing the way consumers purchase tickets. "Ticketless" travel, or automated reservations ticketing, is reducing the need for agents. In addition, many airports now have computerized kiosks that allow passengers to reserve and purchase tickets themselves. Passengers can also access information about fares and flight times on the Internet, where they can also make reservations and purchase tickets. However, for security reasons, all of these services cannot be fully automated, so the need for reservation and transportation ticket agents will never be completely eliminated.

Most openings will occur as experienced agents transfer to other occupations or retire. Competition for jobs is fierce due to declining demand, low turnover, and because of the glamour and attractive travel benefits associated with the industry.

Overall, the transportation industry will remain heavily dependent on the state of the economy. During periods of recession or public fear about the safety of air travel, passenger travel generally declines and transportation companies are less likely to hire new workers, or may even resort to layoffs. The events of September 11, 2001, have greatly affected the transportation industry. In the short term, the general public feared traveling far from home, especially by air, because of threats of further attacks. However, the World Tourism Organization (WTO) predicts that the industry will rebound in the long term. The economic need for business travel—as well as the public's desire for personal travel—will not be permanently altered by external events, according to the WTO.

FOR MORE INFORMATION

For industry and statistical information, as well as to read the Airline Handbook *online, visit ATA's website.*

Air Transport Association
1301 Pennsylvania Avenue, NW
Suite 1100
Washington, DC 20004-1707
Tel: 202-626-4000
Email: ata@airlines.org
http://www.airlines.org

For information on the airline industry, contact
Federal Aviation Administration
800 Independence Avenue, SW
Room 810
Washington, DC 20591
Tel: 202-366-4000
http://www.faa.gov

For information on education, internships, scholarships, or certification in travel and tourism, contact
National Tourism Foundation
546 East Main Street
PO Box 3071
Lexington, KY 40508
Tel: 800-682-8886
Email: ntf@ntastaff.com
http://www.ntfonline.com

For statistics on international travel and tourism, visit the following website:
World Tourism Organization
Capitán Haya 42
28020 Madrid, Spain
Email: omt@world-tourism.org
http://www.world-tourism.org

INTERVIEW

Brynn Starr has worked as a customer support representative for a major airline for five years. She has been with the airline for 10 years. She talked about her career with the editors of Careers in Focus: Aviation.

Q. What are your main and secondary job duties?

A. Most of our customers are internal. We assist customer service agents, reservations customer care representatives, and supervisors along with employees from our headquarters. Our primary job duties are to assist callers with reservation problems. We help the agents at the airport get their passengers boarded on the aircraft, and we help the reservations agents assist our customers on their end. We answer general questions about rules and regulations, fare information, and Internet questions, and we relay information to the appropriate departments when problems arise. Our secondary job duties would include working error queues (which prevents future phone calls to our department) and assisting travel agents and Internet customers.

Q. How/where did you get your first job in this field? What did you do?

A. My first job in the field was as a reservations sales agent in a reservations center. I booked reservations and assisted customers with questions about booking and purchasing air travel on the airline.

Q. What type of training did you receive for this job?

A. I spent five years working in a reservations center, first as an agent for three years and then as a supervisor. My job knowledge and leadership ability helped me to attain my current position. The department in which I currently work offered five weeks of paid training, and then we are continuously trained when new products or procedures are implemented. My original educational path was teaching. Once I started getting promoted within the company, I didn't return to school to finish my degree.

Q. What are the most important qualities for customer support representatives?

A. Patience, good listening skills, the ability to problem solve, and a strong desire to help customers. You should also possess a good work ethic.

Q. What are some of the pros and cons of your job?

A. Pros: flexibility and informality. We are able to trade workdays and shift times with our coworkers, as well as take our vacation time in one-hour increments. Our dress code is extremely relaxed, shorts and t-shirts in the summer, jeans and sweatshirts in the winter. The corporate culture of our company promotes a fun and friendly work environment.

Cons: This job can be very stressful. We are often rushed by our callers and not given the proper credit for fixing their problem. We tend to repeat the same information over and over to different people, which can be frustrating when we feel like the caller is not understanding what we're saying. We spend our entire day on the phones in front of two computers, which is draining.

Q. What advice would you give students who are contemplating a career in this field?

A. Don't go into the airline industry for the money, because you'll be disappointed. The airline that I work for tends to hire for personality and gives training for any skills needed to perform the job. Looking good on paper is one thing, but enthusiasm, commitment, forward thinking, and personality can carry a person pretty far in this industry.

Q. What is the future employment outlook for your job?

A. The airline industry is very volatile, especially since 9/11. My job is pretty secure since we are a specialized area of the company. There is no other department at my airline that does the job we do.

Index

Entries and page numbers in **bold** indicate major treatment of a topic.

A

Accreditation Board for Engineering and Technology (ABET) 18
aerial applicators 26–33
aeronautical and aerospace technicians 4–14
  advancement 10
  aerospace physiological technicians 6
  aircraft launch and recovery technicians 6
  avionics technicians 6
  certification 8
  computer technicians 6
  drafting and design technicians 6
  earnings 11
  electronics technicians 6
  employers 10
  engineering technicians 6
  exploring field 8–10
  high school requirements 7
  history 4–5
  industrial engineering technicians 6
  information 12–14
  instrumentation technicians 7
  job, described 5–7
  liaison technicians 7
  licensing 8
  mathematical technicians 7
  outlook 12
  postsecondary training 7–8
  requirements 7–8
  starting out 10
  target aircraft technicians 7
  work environment 11–12
aerospace engineers 15–25
  advancement 21
  analytical engineers 17
  certification 19
  chief engineer 21
  computational fluid dynamic (CFD) engineers 17
  design aerospace engineers 17
  earnings 21–22
  employers 20
  exploring field 19–20
  high school requirements 18
  history 15–16
  information 24–25
  job, described 16–18
  junior engineer 21
  licensing 19
  manufacturing aerospace engineers 17
  marketing and sales aerospace engineers 17
  materials aerospace engineers 17
  outlook 23
  postsecondary training 18–19
  project engineer 21
  requirements 18–19
  starting out 20–21

top employment sectors and earnings 22
  work environment 22–23
Aerospace Industries Association of America 8
aerospace physiological technicians 6
AgAir Update 31
ag pilots 26–33
Agricultural Aviation 31
agricultural pilots 26–33
  advancement 31
  certification 29
  earnings 32
  employers 31
  exploring field 30–31
  high school requirements 28
  history 26–27
  information 32–33
  job, described 27–28
  licensing 29
  outlook 32
  pesticide, spraying 30
  postsecondary training 29
  requirements 28–30
  starting out 31
  work environment 32
Air Commerce Act 35, 43, 109, 118
aircraft fuelers 132
aircraft launch and recovery technicians 6
aircraft mechanics 34–42
  advancement 40
  aircraft powerplant mechanics 36
  airframe mechanics 36
  avionics technicians 37
  certification 38
  earnings 40–41
  employers 39–40
  exploring field 39
  high school requirements 37
  history 34–35
  information 42
  job, described 35–37
  licensing 38
  line maintenance mechanics 35
  outlook 41–42
  overhaul mechanics 35–36
  postsecondary training 38
  rebuilding plane, illustration 37
  requirements 37–39
  starting out 40
  work environment 41
aircraft powerplant mechanics 36
aircraft servicers 132
airframe mechanics 36
air freight agents 131
Airline Dispatchers Federation 46–49
Air Line Pilots Association 160
airline reservation agents 173
air marshals 51, 53
airplane dispatchers 43–50
  advancement 47–48
  certification 46

183